Country Treasures
Worked in Wood

WOMAN'S DAY®

Country Treasures

Worked in Wood

by the Editors of Woman's Day

Sedgewood® Press

NEW YORK, NEW YORK

For Diamandis Communications Inc.
  EDITORIAL DIRECTOR: Geraldine Rhoads
  PROJECT COORDINATOR: Theresa Capuana
  WRITER/EDITOR: Roslyn Siegel
  CONSULTANT ON INSTRUCTIONS: Lina Morielli
  ADMINISTRATIVE ASSISTANT: Grace Westing
For Sedgewood® Press
  DIRECTOR: Elizabeth P. Rice
  EDITORIAL PROJECT MANAGER: Connie Schrader
  PRODUCTION MANAGER: Bill Rose

Distributed by Meredith Corporation, Des Moines, Iowa

ISBN: 0-696-02325-3
Library of Congress Catalog Card Number: 88-062569

Designed by Stanley S. Drate/Folio Graphics Company, Inc.
Packaged by Rapid Transcript, a division of March Tenth, Inc.

Printed in the United States of America
10 9 8 7 6 5 4 3 2 1

Acknowledgments

Many of the designs in this book were created by the talented men and women who have worked in the Woman's Day Workshop or its Creative Crafts Department. Theresa Capuana, who now heads the latter department, developed many woodcraft projects. Two Workshop directors are particularly remembered for their distinguished work—the late William Whitlock for his early American pieces, typified by the pine accessories in this book, and Albert Strom for designs ranging from sleek modern to classics with the old-time charm of the child's oak heart rocker on page 118.

DESIGNERS:

LORRAINE BODGER: Patchwork Plaque

MARILYN BUDNICK-WEIN: Pretty Planter

BROOKE GREESON: Kitty Catrack

ROBIN GUIDO: Quaint Cottage, Barnyard Mug Holder, Heart Hang-Up, Watermelon Bookshelf

CAROLYN HALL: Whimsical Squirrel, Frisky Raccoon, Friendly Bunny

CHARLES HAALAND: Racing Horse Mantel Mount

LINA MORIELLI: Dollhouse Side Cabinet (from an idea by Gary Brouwer), Chief Chef Herb and Spice Shelf, Picket Fence Plate Rack, Blooming Hose Holder, "I Love America" Heart, Country Landscape, Show-off Plant Shelf, Old-Fashioned Onion and Garlic Keeper, Spice Space.

LEE RENNER: Marmalade Cat Mug Holder, Wonderful Welcome, Autumn Acorn Shutter Trim, Gossiping Geese, Pineapple Nameplate, Purrs for the Postman

CAL SACKS: Cock-of-the-Walk, Tavern Sign, Rooster Weather Vane

PHOTOGRAPHERS:

FRANCES PELLEGRINI: Heart Rocker

PHOTOGRAPHY HOUSE: Versatile Spoon Rack, Dressing Table Caddy, Handsome Twosome: Cabinet and Rack.

CARMEN SCHIAVONE: Happy Baby Low Chair

WILLIAM SEITZ: Painted Wall "Quilt"

The Woman's Day Photographic Studio is responsible for all other photos: Ben Calvo, chief photographer.

Contents

Introduction

At *Woman's Day* magazine we have always taken special pride in designing wonderful wood-working projects for our readers. Nothing has quite the warmth of wood, the unique graining and rich markings that result from the alternation of seasons. Nothing else so suggests the beauty of nature, the fertility of our fruitful country, our American heritage.

Americans have always had a love affair with wood. Our forefathers were accomplished weavers, silversmiths, and potters, but above all, they were skilled carpenters and wood-workers. The vast forests of the country provided a natural resource that was truly spectacular by any standard. The wood that was cleared for homesteading was used to build the colonial home itself, and each home in turn was filled with wood—wood floors, wood paneling, and of course, wood furniture.

As Americans forged a national identity, they also created a national style: the unpainted log cabin; the brightly colored, white-shuttered farmhouse; the Southern plantation home with its stately white columns and porch. On the frontier, furniture might be rough-hewn pine, a style we call rustic today. In more established settlements, it might be birch or maple, modeled after the sleek, spare lines introduced by the Shakers. In the wealthiest, most sophisticated areas, it might be the carved, curved cherry or mahogany pieces we call Federal. The texture, color, and graining of the wood enhanced the feeling of the finished piece—from the mysterious dark glow of polished pine to the sunny amber lights of cherry and the cool, pale satin of birch.

As we have become more and more aware of our colonial heritage, we have found a new regard for the furniture and the folk art of our ancestors. And the pages of *Woman's Day* have reflected that interest. Although casual country-style furniture has always been popular in America, now it seems as if even the cities have gone country. Contemporary small floral prints and country colors—forest green, slate blue, barn red—so popular today, are a marvelous backdrop for the accessories we love.

Many homes already have a small workshop tucked away in the basement or the garage. Some apartment dwellers have even set up a workspace in their closets. But today, wood-working needn't take up much room. Technology has made small power tools available and women, as well as men, are operating them safely and easily.

Our designs in wood have always had a colonial flavor. Now we have searched through our files to pluck out our favorites—our own Country Treasures. They range from a graceful plant shelf to a majestic country hutch, from a cozy baby cradle to a whimsical kitty key rack. You'll find delightful decorations and we-mean-business practical projects. Some you will want to give away to lucky friends and loved ones as gifts; others you'll never want to part with. All of them are derived from an authentic colonial or country design, and none of them requires more than hand or small power tools. To make the most of everyone's budget, we use a great deal of pine plywood, even wood scraps. But there's no compromise in the results. Pine has a marvelous rugged look, rich graining—and it's soft enough to cut easily.

Our stencil designs, diagrams, and easy directions will make these instant antiques a breeze to create. Some you will be able to complete within a few hours. Others may take a bit longer. So clear a space at your work table—your kitchen table may do—and experience the joy of creating your own handmade country treasures.

LITTLE
TREASURES

Here are accent pieces that spell HOME—the small touches that express old-time comfort and warmth. Again and again, they were inspired by the useful and decorative items our forefathers made for themselves.

These "instant antiques" would cost a bundle if you found them in a shop. Make them yourself and give your own descendants heirlooms to cherish.

ALL-SEASON HEARTH ACCENTS

This lively group invites the right climate for indoor or outdoor pastimes: The rooster's arrow points to fair weather for all-season walking, the game board and letters suggest lovely hours toasting by the fire or enjoying a hint of a breeze from an open window.

ROOSTER WEATHER VANE

SIZE:
Approximately 16½″ wide × 2′ high

MATERIALS:
1′ of 1 × 12 pine
1′ of 1 × 8 pine
1½′ of ½ × 4 pine
⅜″-diameter dowel
Primer
Artist's acrylic paints: orange, red, yellow, blue, and black
Acrylic polymer medium and acrylic burnt umber for
    antique finish
Glossy black spray paint
White glue

TOOLS:
Brushes No. 5 and No. 8, rasp, coping saw, drill, chisel,
round file, clamp

Following General Directions, enlarge patterns, omitting shaping lines; trace rooster on ¾″ pine and arrow on ½″ pine. Cut out.

Drill hole for dowel in rooster. Taper and round shaded areas of rooster with rasp, narrowing beak and wattle further for definition.

Prime, then paint rooster orange and beak red. Use quick, spontaneous strokes to paint feathers (see photograph), using No. 5 brush for neck, breast, and tail and No. 8 brush for wings.

Cut dowel to 14¼″. Cut 6½″ × 12″ base from 1 × 8 pine; bevel edges.

To fasten arrow to dowel, make a ⅛″-deep half-round notch midway in arrow using round file. Glue arrow to dowel about 5″ from one end. Clamp and let dry. Spray-paint dowel, arrow, and base black. Drill hole through center of base; assemble with glue. Antique finish (see General Directions).

Each sq. = ½″

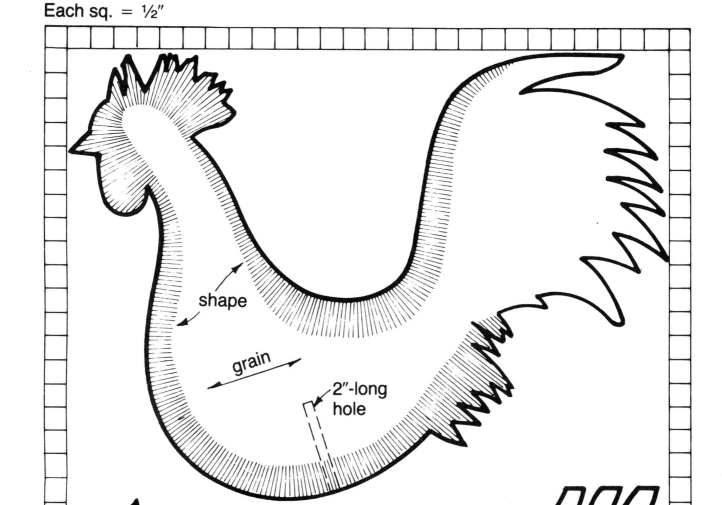

shape

grain

2″-long hole

16½″ total length

SIZES:
8″ high, 6¼″ high, 5″ high

MATERIALS:
2′ of 1 × 10 pine
Artist's acrylic paints: yellow ocher, dark green, blue-gray,
    rust, black

TOOLS:
Coping or saber saw

Enlarge patterns, following General Directions. Trace letters on pine. Cut letters on heavy outside lines.

To paint, follow color in photograph, mixing colors (except rust) with water to consistency of stain; brush color on over entire letter; wipe off; repeat to desired shade. Then, using full-strength rust, paint areas indicated.

Each sq. = 1″

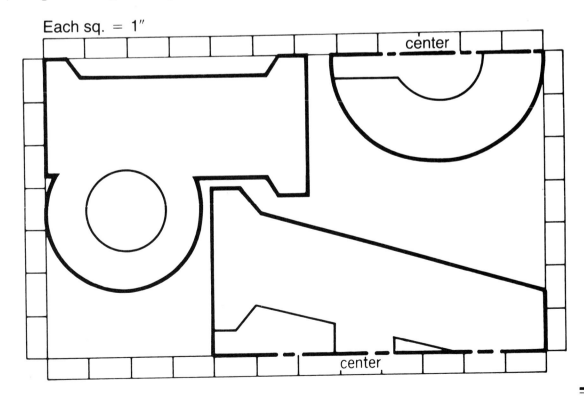

SIZE:
16″ square

MATERIALS:
16″-square piece of ¾″ plywood
6′ of ½″ picture molding
Artist's acrylic paints: white, burnt umber, crimson,
    green, blue
Spackle
Primer
Brads

TOOLS:
Miter box, saw, sandpaper, masking tape

Cut four 16″ lengths of picture molding with mitered corners. Tack molding to top of board, sinking brads. Spackle sides and holes; sand smooth.

Prime surfaces to be painted. Paint board white tinted with burnt umber. Let dry.

Mark off 12″ square in center with masking tape; draw grid of 1½″ squares in marked-off area. Paint every other square blue.

Mask off ⅛″-wide strip around checkerboard for inner border; paint green. Paint outer border crimson and frame green. Antique finish, following General Directions.

COUNTRY
FAIR
MANTEL

The galloping horse will spirit the flavor of Americana right into your living room. He makes a perfect complement to the staid patchwork wooden plaque, with its pieces painted in acrylic paint and put together like a puzzle.

PATCHWORK PLAQUE

SIZE:
Approximately 14″ square

MATERIALS:
13″ square piece of ¼″ plywood
8′ of ¼″ × 2⅝″ lattice
5′ of ⅝″ × ⅞″ strip for frame
Artist's acrylic paints: green, blue, gold, burnt sienna,
    brown
White glue
1″ brads

TOOLS:
Saw, sandpaper, brushes, rags

For backing, use 13″ plywood square. From lattice strip, cut twelve 3⅝″ × 3⅝″ × 5″ triangles and eight parallelograms, 3⅝″ on each side. (You will be cutting the lattice strip on a diagonal line across measuring 3⅝″ from edge to edge.)

For stained look, follow photograph for colors, and with a brush apply acrylic paint thinned with water to each piece, then wipe off. Let dry, then apply second coat in same way. If necessary, lightly sand.

Arrange and glue pieces to the square of ¼″ plywood trimmed to fit.

For frame, cut ⅝″ × ⅞″ strip to fit outer edges, mitering corners. Stain and glue in place.

RACING HORSE MANTEL MOUNT

SIZE:
18″ wide × 16″ high

MATERIALS:
1½′ of 1 × 12 pine
Red and walnut stain
8″ piece of ⅜″ dowel
2½″ × 2½″ × 9″ scrap lumber
White glue

TOOLS:
Coping saw, drill, 1″ brush, rag

Enlarge pattern, following General Directions. Trace and cut out horse from pine. Apply red stain, then create distressed antiqued look, following General Directions.

Cut dowel to 7″. From 2½″ × 2½″ scrap lumber, cut base with tapered ends, with 9″ along bottom and 6″ at top. Stain dowel and base walnut.

Drill ⅜″ hole through horse's head for eye. Drill ⅜″ holes ½″ deep in center bottom of horse and top of base. Assemble with glue.

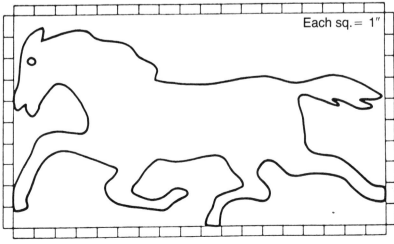

Each sq. = 1″

COMFY
FOOTREST

Just looking at this charming footstool makes you want to relax. Slanted legs give it stability, and it's made with an oval-shaped top, a perfect place for a pillow—and your tired feet.

SIZE:
Approximately 12″ wide × 6½″ high × 7½″ deep

MATERIALS:
1′ of 1 × 8 pine
2′ of ½ × 8 pine
Two 1¼″ × ⅜″ dowels
Cotton batting
½ yard each of muslin and fabric
1 yard of welting cord
Upholsterer's tacks
1¼″ No. 8 flathead wood screws
White glue
Pine stain
Artist's acrylic paint: burnt umber

TOOLS:
Coping and saber saws, plane, drill, depth gauge

Enlarge pattern, following General Directions. Follow pattern to cut legs from 1″ pine. Cut and bevel stretcher and legs as in diagram. Glue pieces together and drill a ⅜″ hole through each leg, using an adjustable bit gauge set for 1¼″ depth. Glue in dowels.

Follow pattern for top; temporarily nail two pieces of ½″ wood together and mark outer and inner ovals on top piece. Cut through both pieces on outer line and separate pieces. To cut out platform and rim, drill a ⅜″ hole near inner line and begin at hole to saw around inner line; plug hole with a dowel.

To upholster platform, cover it with a layer of cotton batting, smoothing out edges. Place muslin and fabric over batting as in diagram and tack to underside. Cut remaining fabric into 2″-wide bias strips and join to make one long strip to fit around platform. Fold and stitch over welting cord; tack around platform.

Test-fit platform inside the rim. Sand the rim if necessary to enlarge opening. Glue rim in place and screw seat to legs and stretcher. Apply antique pine finish, following General Directions. Screw covered platform to seat with two or more screws.

ASSEMBLY DIAGRAM

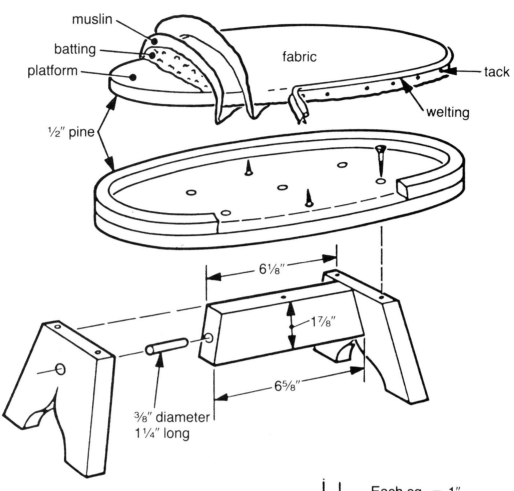

muslin

batting

platform

½″ pine

fabric

tack

welting

6⅛″

1⅞″

6⅝″

⅜″ diameter
1¼″ long

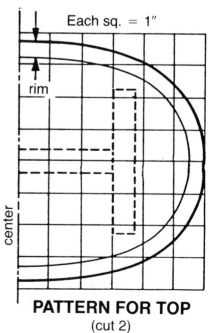

Each sq. = 1″

rim

center

PATTERN FOR TOP
(cut 2)

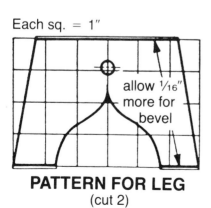

Each sq. = 1″

allow 1/16″
more for
bevel

PATTERN FOR LEG
(cut 2)

PAINTED WALL "QUILT"

This wooden "quilt" is even brighter and bolder than the item that inspired it, and you never have to mend it. The base is made of plywood and the design is created from precut purchased wooden hearts and triangles.

First lay out your picture. Since your triangles may differ in size from ours, lay them out following the photograph before cutting your backing material, lattice, and moldings. Adjust shapes to fit—placement can be slightly loose or irregular. Sand edges for small adjustments if necessary.

Measure center square, corners, and outside dimension, allowing for eventual placement of lattice and corner moldings to frame edge. Cut backing, lattice, and molding to fit.

Now paint all elements. In separate cups mix blue paint with dab of gray, red with burnt sienna, yellow with burnt sienna; thin each slightly with water.

Tape corners, and with a dampened sponge, paint-stain the corners and thirty-six triangles yellow. Let corners dry. Cover edges and flat surfaces evenly, allowing some wood grain to show through. To get an even coat, do not add color after paint begins to dry. Tape again and paint-stain remainder of board blue. Paint-stain remaining triangles, hearts, lattice, and molding red. Let dry.

With glue, attach lattice and moldings to backing. Weight with heavy books; let dry one hour or more. Picking up pieces one at a time, hot-glue shapes in place. Attach two sawtooth hangers to back of plywood.

STURDY STEP STOOL

This triangular step stool is as trustworthy as it is attractive. Now you can reach those high shelves in style. Adapted from an Early American design, it is worked in pine for long-lasting service.

SIZE:
16½" wide × 7½" high × 9½" deep

MATERIALS:
6' of 1 × 10 pine
1½" finishing nails
Wood filler
Primer
Polyurethane varnish
White glue
¾"-diameter glides

TOOLS:
Saber saw, clamps, sandpaper

Enlarge side pattern, following General Directions. Transfer shape to pine or hardwood and cut out two sides, using fine-toothed saber-saw blade to cut curves.

Following assembly diagram, mark and cut out two each of lower and upper end pieces with 45° angled cuts along one 9½" edge of each. These pieces must fit on side pieces as indicated. Also cut out top and inside oval, following General Directions.

To assemble stool, glue and partially nail sides and lower ends together so there is ¼" overhang on each side. Check that assembly is square and that bottom edges are flush to each other. Drive in nails; clamp. Add upper ends and top.

Set all nails and fill holes with wood filler. Remove clamps. Sand stool smooth, slightly breaking edges. Dust. Apply a primer coat of polyurethane; sand lightly when dry. Apply finish coat of polyurethane; let dry. Add glides in corners.

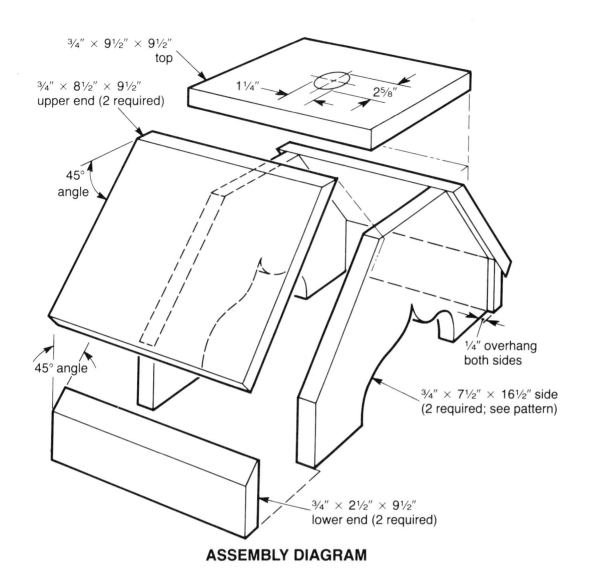

¾" × 9½" × 9½" top

¾" × 8½" × 9½" upper end (2 required)

45° angle

45° angle

1¼"

2⅝"

¼" overhang both sides

¾" × 7½" × 16½" side (2 required; see pattern)

¾" × 2½" × 9½" lower end (2 required)

ASSEMBLY DIAGRAM

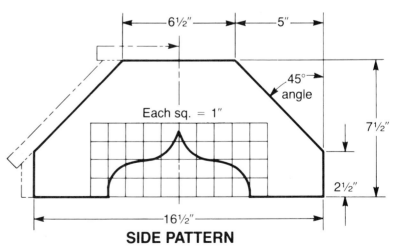

6½"

5"

45° angle

Each sq. = 1"

7½"

2½"

16½"

SIDE PATTERN

SEAFARER'S FIRESIDE

Who needs expensive antiques when you can make nostalgic accessories like these? Use a stencil to paint this square-rigger tavern sign. The shorebird decoy is made of pine and dowels. Its color will remind you of the sea. The standing heart and half apples just require painting over wood scraps, but they make an eye-catching group of color and shape.

STANDING
HEART

SIZE:
About 5½″ wide × 8″ high

MATERIALS:
5″ × 6″ piece of ¼″ plywood
6″ of ¼″ × 1⅜″ lattice
Two 4½″ lengths of ¾″ × ¾″ strips
Artist's acrylic paints: dark red and green
White glue
Polyurethane varnish

TOOLS:
Coping or saber saw

Make heart pattern 4½″ long × 5½″ wide. (You can adapt the pattern used for the "I Love America" Heart on page 90.) Cut heart from plywood.

Paint heart and lattice strips. Let dry. Glue heart to vertical support. For base, glue one end of vertical support between the two ¾″ strips. Coat with polyurethane.

TAVERN SIGN

SIZE:
Approximately 24½″ wide × 15″ high

MATERIALS:
4′ of 1 × 8 No. 2 pine
14⅝″ × 24″ piece of hardboard or ¼″ plywood for
   backing
8½′ each of ¼″-round molding and ¼″ × 1⅜″ lattice for
   frame
2″ alphabet stencils (optional)
Artist's acrylic paint: white, raw sienna, black, yellow
   ocher, light cadmium red, ultramarine blue, light
   blue, green, burnt umber
White glue
Acrylic gesso
Screws
Brads

TOOLS:
Hand saw, miter box, flat and pointed brushes, paper and
carbon paper

Each sq. = 1″

To prepare board and frame: From pine cut two 7¼″ × 24″ pieces. Attach to backing, using glue and brads, leaving ⅛″ joint in center. Cut molding, mitering corners, to fit around top of panel flush with edge. Cut lattice to fit around outer edge. (Do not attach frame until painting has been completed.) Coat front of panel and frame pieces with gesso, leaving brush marks.

To paint: Cover entire panel with light blue mixed with a touch of green. Let dry. Enlarge design and transfer (see General Directions) to painted background with carbon paper, omitting stenciled letters and scrolls.

Following photograph, paint picture, shading and modeling sails and allowing touch of blue background to show through. Paint green base, omitting letters and scrolls. When surface is dry, stencil "Tavern," following General Directions, then add scroll motifs. Paint and attach frame (we used black for lattice, red-sienna for molding).

When sign is completely dry, create distressed look and apply antique finish, following General Directions.

SIZE:
Approximately 15″ wide × 24″ high

MATERIALS:
Two 1′ lengths of 2 × 4 building studs (free of knots) for
    body (glue and clamp two pieces together)
½″-diameter dowel
7″ of 1 × 8 pine for base
Primer
White glue, pine stain
Artist's acrylic paints: yellow, blue, and burnt umber
Acrylic polymer medium

TOOLS:
Coping saw, drill, pocket knife, chisel or rasp, clamp

From dowel cut 10″ leg, 8½″ neck, and 5½″ beak. From block of wood, carve and shape body, head, and beak with pocket knife, chisel, and/or rasp (a saw can be used to take off large amounts of wood). Leave all marks and gouges for a handmade look. (Use photograph as a guide to rough shape desired.)

Fashion head from scrap wood about 1⅛″ in diameter. Drill ½″-diameter and 3/16″-diameter holes for neck and beak. Taper beak to point and whittle down to a 3/16″-diameter peg on other end; glue peg into head. Follow photograph to determine angles for leg and neck holes in body.

Prime. Let dry. Then, using acrylics, paint body, neck, and head blue, beak and leg yellow. Let dry; antique (see General Directions). Stain base with pine stain. Drill hole in center of base for leg; assemble with glue.

HALF
APPLES

SIZE:
3½″ wide × 4″ high

MATERIALS:
1′ of 1 × 4 pine
Artist's acrylic paints: red, green, light yellow, orange,
    black
Polyurethane varnish

TOOLS:
Coping or saber saw, sandpaper

Enlarge pattern, following General Directions. Trace and cut apples from pine. Sand edges.

Paint the pieces, following photograph for color scheme. (Thin paint slightly with water and brush on.) Let dry. Coat with polyurethane.

Each sq. = 1″

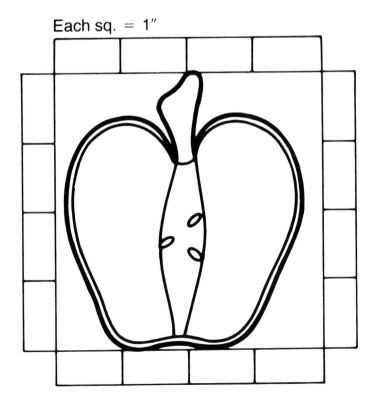

COUNTRY
KEEPERS

Our lives are so full of things we cherish . . . not to mention all the appurtenances that make life easier. Here, then, are attractive ways to house some of these treasures, ranging from keepers in the Early American tradition to holders that express our contemporary needs.

DOLLHOUSE SIDE CABINET

The most delectable little side cabinet we can imagine is practical, too. The front panel opens, and there's an inner shelf for storing things. Paint it to match your decor.

SIZE:
19¾" wide × 25¼" high × 15¼" deep

MATERIALS:
4' × 4' piece of ½" birch plywood
2' × 2' piece of ¼" birch plywood
6' each of solid crown moldings
 Top trim 1⅛" × 1¾"
 Bottom trim ¹¹⁄₁₆" × 1⅜"
1½" finishing nails
White glue
One pair ½" × 2" butt hinges with screws
Wood filler
Primer
White and beige satin enamel
Artist's acrylic paints: beige, medium gray, light gray
Magnetic catch

TOOLS:
Miter box, saw, sandpaper, 1" flat paintbrush, ½" and 1" masking tapes

Cut following pieces from ½" birch plywood: sides, 12½" × 23¼"; top and bottom, each 13" × 17½"; back, 16½" × 23¼"; shelf, 12" × 16½"; door, 17½" × 21½". From ¼" birch plywood cut second top, 15" × 19½".

Construct basic cabinet with glue and finishing nails. Assemble three-sided box from sides and back. Center shelf inside. Nail in place.

Cut and miter moldings to fit around sides at top and bottom. Glue and nail top molding flush with upper edge. Turn bottom moldings upside down and attach ½" flush with top surface of bottom plywood (moldings extend below cabinet).

Hinge door in place at right side of front. Glue and nail second top set ⅛" to ¼" from edges of top molding. Sink nails; fill holes. Sand. Prime. Let dry. Sand again. Paint cabinet with two coats of white.

Enlarge and cut out window pattern (see "How to Enlarge Patterns" in General Directions). Trace three windows on cabinet front and extend pattern to trace 10" door. Trace two windows each on cabinet sides. Place 1"-wide masking tape along vertical edges (including edge of door on left); place ½"-wide tape along top. Tape top edge of bottom molding. Mask white areas of windows with tape or self-adhesive plastic. Paint background and windowpanes as shown in photograph. Remove tape. Attach magnetic catch for door.

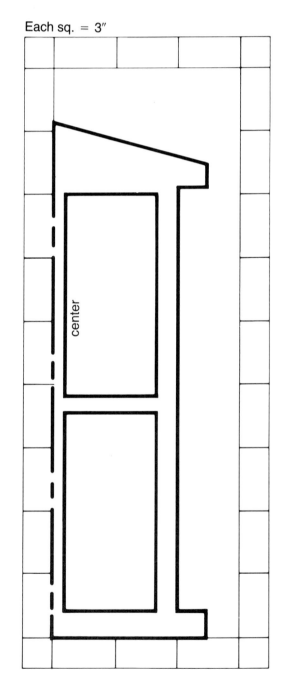

Each sq. = 3"

center

SCALLOPED
SALT BOX

This colonial-style salt box will flavor any kitchen. Its decorative back and flat bottom make it equally suitable for hanging on the wall or standing on a table.

SIZE:
7½″ wide at base × 11½″ high × 4¾″ deep

MATERIALS:
4′ of ½ × 8 pine
¼″ dowel
White glue
Pine stain
Artist's acrylic paint: burnt umber

TOOLS:
Drill, rasp, coping saw, plane, sandpaper

Following General Directions, follow pattern to cut back, and drill hole. Follow diagram to cut sides and front; attach sides to front and back.

Bevel front to angle of sides and attach base. Cut lid, beveling and rounding as in diagram.

Drill a ¼″ hole in each side of lid to ⅜″ depth. Drill ⁵⁄₁₆″ holes through sides. Temporarily insert dowels and test lid for clearance when opening; plane and sand lid, if necessary. Glue dowels to lid only, following General Directions for dowels.

Sand the box, rounding corners and edges. Apply antique pine stain, following General Directions.

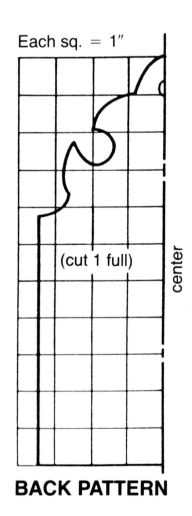

Each sq. = 1″

(cut 1 full)

center

BACK PATTERN

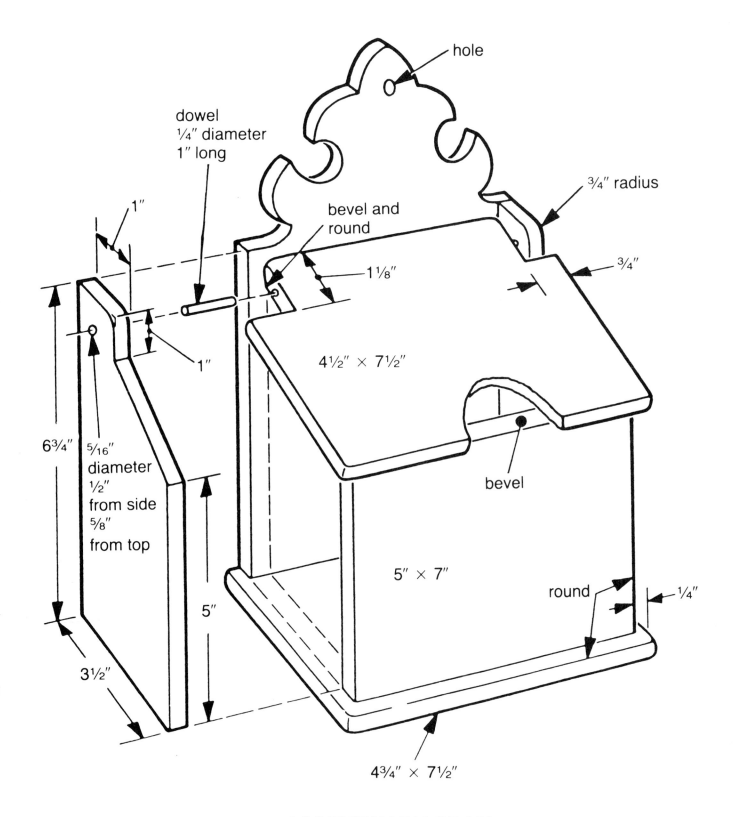

hole

dowel
¼" diameter
1" long

¾" radius

1"

bevel and
round

1⅛"

¾"

4½" × 7½"

1"

bevel

6¾"

⁵⁄₁₆"
diameter
½"
from side
⅝"
from top

5"

5" × 7"

round

¼"

3½"

4¾" × 7½"

ASSEMBLY DIAGRAM

43

KITTY CATRACK

Who says cats can't be trained to do tricks? Our tiger "catrack" is a whiz at holding several sets of keys at once. Paint the "keyboard" a bright color so you'll never lose track of your keys again.

SIZE:
6½″ wide × 3½″ high

MATERIALS:
4″ × 7″ piece of ¼″ plywood
Six cup hooks
Primer
Artist's acrylic paints: yellow, red, black, white, turquoise
Sawtooth hanger

TOOLS:
Sandpaper, small pointed and flat paintbrushes, coping or saber saw, carbon paper

Enlarge pattern, following General Directions. Trace outline onto plywood; cut out. Sand smooth. Prime; let dry.

Transfer details to front with carbon paper. Paint front and edges, following photograph for colors.

Attach hanger to back. Screw hooks to front on border.

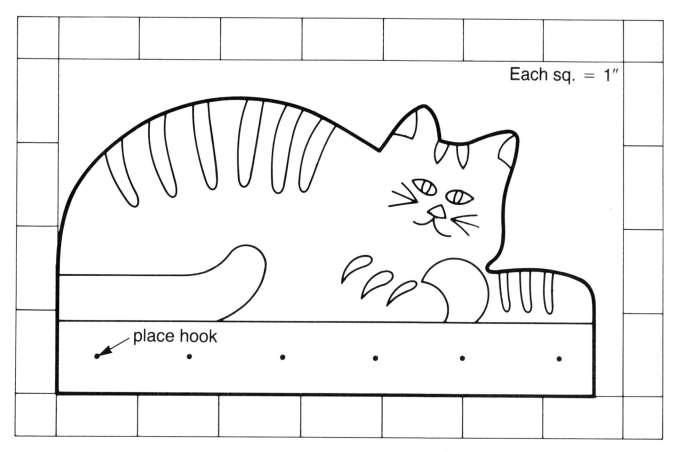

Each sq. = 1″

place hook

MARMALADE CAT MUG HOLDER

This cat helps out in the kitchen. Our charming hang-up is cut from pine, painted, and fitted with pegs. Use it to show off your prettiest mugs.

SIZE:
21" wide × 16" high

MATERIALS:
2' of 1 × 8 pine
2' of 1 × 10 pine
Four 2¾"-long Shaker pegs with ½"-diameter tenon (or
    four 3½"-long × ½"-diameter dowels)
White glue
White primer
Artist's acrylic paints: sage green, terra cotta, warm
    brown, black, gold, red

TOOLS:
Rasp, coping saw, sandpaper, 1½"-wide masking tape,
drill with ½"-diameter bit, clamps, large and small
pointed and flat brushes, craft knife, carbon paper, clamp

Glue two pieces of pine together, long edge to long edge. Clamp together and let dry.

Enlarge pattern, following General Directions. Transfer outline and peg positions to wood with carbon paper. Cut outline. Round front edges with rasp. Sand smooth. Drill holes for pegs. Insert pegs. Prime front, sides, and pegs. Remove pegs.

Transfer details of cat, omitting facial features and painting entire checkerboard gold. Paint as many coats as needed, letting paint dry between coats. Transfer and paint facial features.

Cover checkerboard strip with masking tape. Transfer squares from pattern to tape. Cut out every other square with craft knife. Paint exposed squares red. Remove remaining tape. Insert pegs, gluing in place.

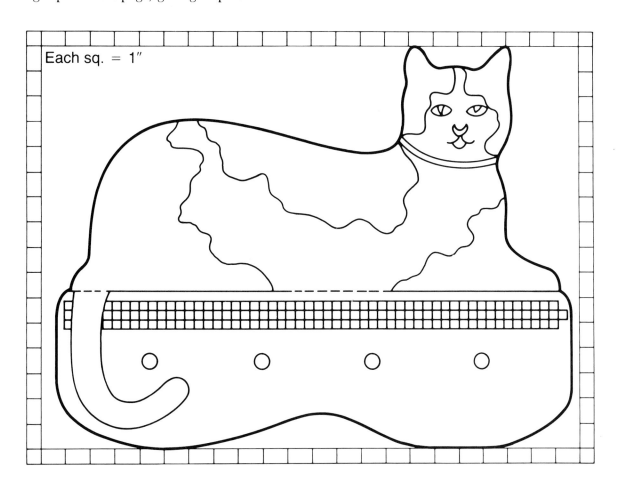

Each sq. = 1″

SPACIOUS SPICE BOXES

Sugar and spice and everything nice . . . With their hinged scalloped and roomy insides, these spice boxes make handy containers for the most adventurous cook—or the most traditional.

SIZES:
5" wide × 6½" high × 4" deep
6" wide × 7" high × 5" deep
7" wide × 7½" high × 6" deep

MATERIALS:
12' of ½ × 8 pine
Six ¾" cabinet hinges with screws
White glue
Pine stain
Brads

TOOLS:
Rasp, saw, plane, sandpaper

To make small, medium, and large boxes, see chart for individual dimensions keyed to letters in diagram.

Glue and nail pieces together, beveling front to angle of sides and rounding edges (see General Directions). Notch top for hinges and round edges; glue and nail in place.

Follow patterns to cut lid for each box. Round edges as in side view and notch for hinges. Sand well and apply antique pine stain, following General Directions. Hinge lid to top of box.

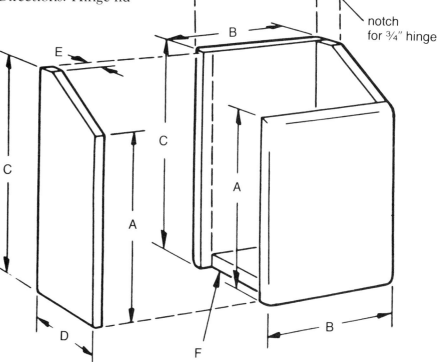

notch for ¾" hinge

ASSEMBLY DIAGRAM

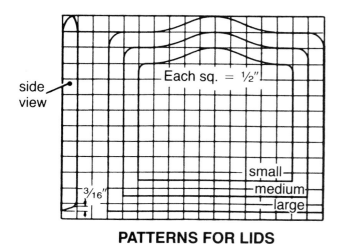

side view

Each sq. = ½"

small
medium
large

3/16"

PATTERNS FOR LIDS

MEASUREMENTS CHART

Size	A	B	C	D	E	F	G	H	J
small	$5\frac{1}{2}$"	5"	$6\frac{1}{2}$"	4"	1"	4 x 4"	$1\frac{1}{2}$"x 5"	$\frac{1}{2}$"	$4\frac{1}{4}$"x 5"
medium	6"	6"	7"	5"	$1\frac{1}{4}$"	5 x 5"	$1\frac{3}{4}$"x 6"	$\frac{3}{4}$"	$5\frac{1}{4}$"x 6"
large	$6\frac{1}{2}$"	7"	$7\frac{1}{2}$"	6"	$1\frac{1}{2}$"	6 x 6"	2"x 7"	1"	$6\frac{1}{4}$"x 7"

HEAVY-DUTY DOUGH BOX

We have scaled down this dough box to keep the country look and make it useful for other things. It's a splendid place to keep wooden spoons and other utensils. Make it out of common pine. Distress it to give an antique glow, and finish with stain and polyurethane.

SIZE:
19½" wide × 6¼" high × 7½" deep

MATERIALS:
8' of 1 × 8 pine
1½" finishing nails
Two 1¼" flathead screws
White glue
Pine stain
Polyurethane varnish
Paste wax

TOOLS:
Rasp, saber saw, plane, sandpaper, steel wool

Enlarge pattern, following General Directions. Cut bottom, sides, and ends. Round bottom edges slightly. With plane, cut bevels and angles on top and bottom edges of sides and ends. Test-fit.

Plane end grain of side pieces at slight angle to abut ends. Glue and nail sides, ends, and bottom.

Cut 1½″ × 7″ box handles. Cut curve on handle to follow end curve; glue to ends. Shape outside curve with rasp.

Cut lid with beveled edges to fit inside box; sand smooth. Sand sharp edges of handle; screw to lid. Round all edges heavily with sandpaper. Stain and when dry finish with polyurethane and paste wax, following General Directions.

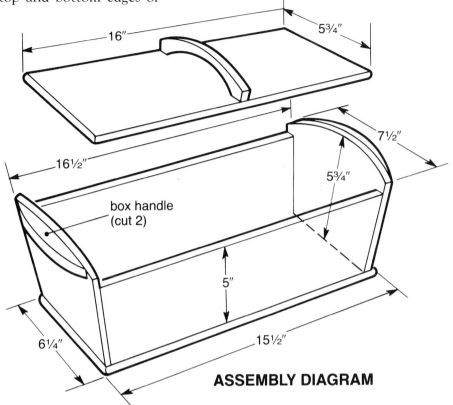

ASSEMBLY DIAGRAM

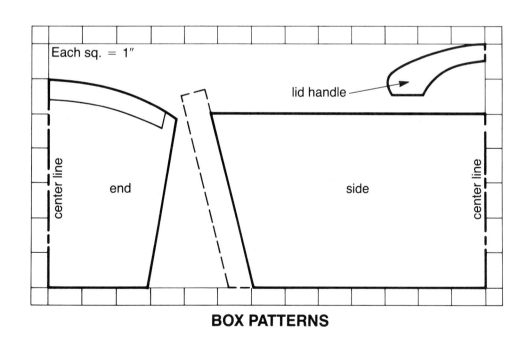

BOX PATTERNS

GRANDPA'S
TOOLBOX

This old-time toolbox is ideal for keeping tableware together. It is large enough for a whole family's forks, spoons, and knives—serving pieces, too. It has one partition and a two-part hinged cover to keep everything clean and orderly.

SIZE:
14¼" wide × 4" high × 10½" deep

MATERIALS:
1' of 1 × 2 pine
6' of ½ × 4 pine
5' of ½ × 6 pine
Two pairs of ¾" × 1" hinges with screws
1" No. 6 flathead screws
Pine stain

TOOLS:
Drill, saw, sandpaper, chisel

Enlarge pattern for handle, following cutting pattern and General Directions. Transfer pattern to 1 × 2 pine and cut out. Cut following from ½ × 4 pine: two sides, each 3" × 9"; front and back, each 3" × 13¾"; fixed top, 2" × 14¼". From ½ × 6 pine, cut two hinged tops, each 4¼" × 14¼", and two bottoms, each 5¼" × 14¼".

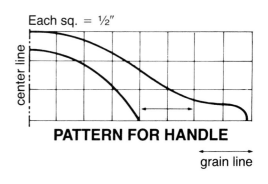

Each sq. = ½"

center line

PATTERN FOR HANDLE

grain line

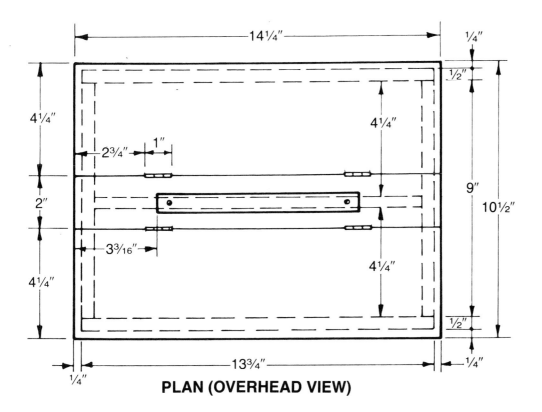

PLAN (OVERHEAD VIEW)

Following General Directions, mortise for hinges on fixed top piece only (do not cut mortises deeper than the thickness of the hinge when closed). Drill handle for screws. Assemble the sides and bottom; add partition.

Attach fixed top. Attach handle. Attach hinges to mortises and to hinged top pieces.

To finish, apply pine stain, following General Directions.

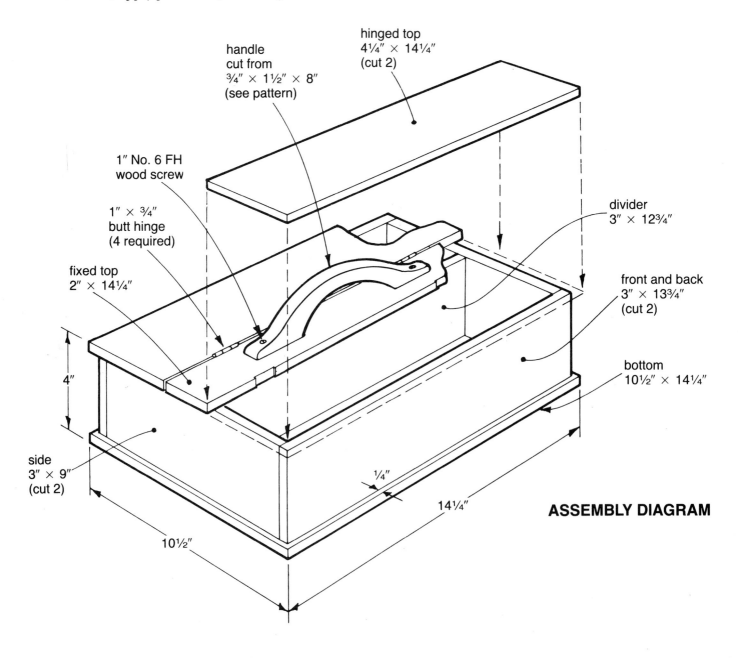

handle
cut from
¾″ × 1½″ × 8″
(see pattern)

hinged top
4¼″ × 14¼″
(cut 2)

1″ No. 6 FH
wood screw

1″ × ¾″
butt hinge
(4 required)

fixed top
2″ × 14¼″

divider
3″ × 12¾″

front and back
3″ × 13¾″
(cut 2)

bottom
10½″ × 14¼″

side
3″ × 9″
(cut 2)

4″

¼″

14¼″

10½″

ASSEMBLY DIAGRAM

OLD-FASHIONED ONION AND GARLIC KEEPER

This sweetheart of a box with its heart-shaped windows captures the charm of a French country kitchen. It will hold your onions and garlic neatly, and a quick peek will tell you when to buy some more.

Cut following pieces with grain running horizontally: *front* 4⅞″ × 11½″, *back* 9½″ × 12½″, *two sides* 5¾″ wide × 6⅜″ high, *lid* 5½″ × 11½″, *bottom* 4⅞″ × 11⁹⁄₁₆″ (cut bottom last and trim to fit inside box).

Enlarge pattern, following General Directions. Trace curves, hearts, and holes on appropriate pieces. Cut out heart shapes as described in General Directions; drill holes with ½″ bit. Cut curves. Sand all shaped edges smooth.

Assemble box with glue and brads. (*Note:* Front and back fit between sides.) Cut bottom to fit; glue and nail. Sink nail heads and fill holes with wood filler. Sand all surfaces smooth.

To hinge lid, first measure ¼″ from top edge and ½″ from inside back and mark location on each side of box. Drill hole same size as brad (or fraction larger) through sides where marked. Position lid on box (sand lid if fit is too snug) so that it is flush with top edges of sides and ⅛″ from back, then wedge cardboard or toothpicks between lid and back to hold placement. Turn box on side and nail brad through side into lid; repeat for other side.

Finish wood with polyurethane.

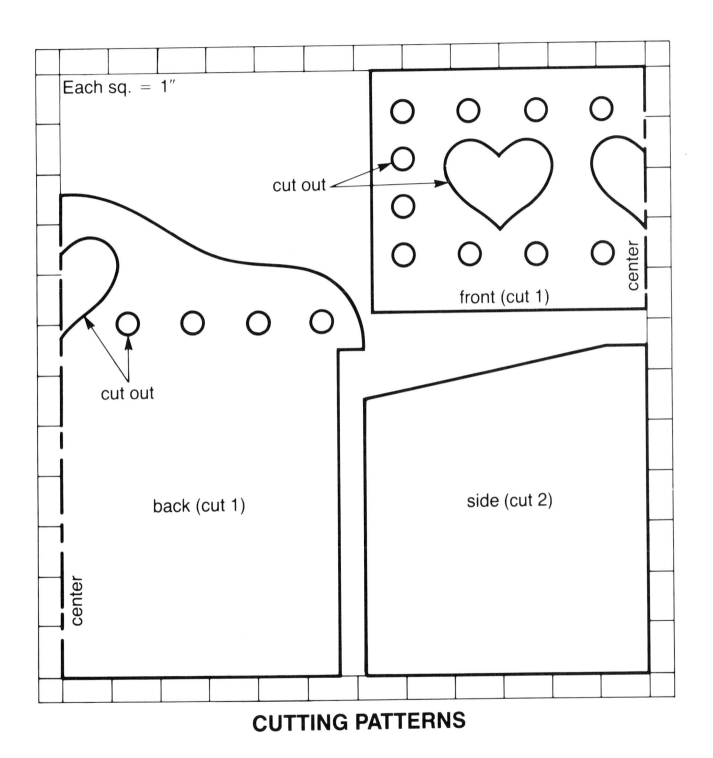

Each sq. = 1″

cut out

cut out

front (cut 1)

center

cut out

back (cut 1)

side (cut 2)

center

CUTTING PATTERNS

HANG-UPS

Whoever invented shelves should go down in history as one of civilization's great benefactors—a VIP to all of us with treasures to show off or miscellany to hide discreetly. This chapter offers delightful interpretations of the ever-practical shelf. The wonder here is that so many of our hang-ups are really so easy to make. They range from traditional colonial pieces to more contemporary "country."

In the first category are the pine accessories designed to look like generations-old family hand-me-downs. They're all antiqued, distressed, and stained. A mistake or two just adds to their "authentic" charm.

We also include items you can put together with some scraps of wood and finish with stain or bright-colored paint to achieve great country-color looks.

COUNTRY-STYLE "HUTCH"

Here's a dramatic way to dress up a base cabinet and expand your display space at the same time. And it's so easy to put together! Just paint the wall above the cabinet and frame it with a wallpaper border. Then cut shelves the same width as the cabinet and mount them on brackets within the pretty framework. It's a knockout look and much less costly than a real hutch.

SIZE:
Make shelves same length as your existing cabinet.

MATERIALS:
1 × 10 pine shelving (to run length of existing cabinet)
1"-thick decorative unfinished wooden brackets with
    keyhole slot for hanging
Stain (to match cabinet)
Wallpaper border

TOOLS:
Level, saber saw, sandpaper

Decide size of wall to be covered and then paint wall (see photograph). With level and light pencil, draw two vertical lines on the wall about 1" in from sides of cabinet. At top of area, draw horizontal connecting line to complete "frame." Apply border around frame, mitering corners.

Cut shelves to fit within frame. Sand and stain shelves and brackets. Following instructions on package, attach brackets to wall. Set shelves on brackets.

NOOK-AND-CRANNY SPICE RACK

This is the most complicated of our country keepers, with drawers and doors. But don't worry. An ill fit here or there is just part of the authentic look.

Enlarge patterns for sides and center divider, following General Directions, and transfer to wood. Cut all parts, following diagrams. Fill edges of plywood back.

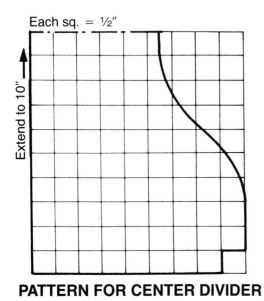

PATTERN FOR CENTER DIVIDER

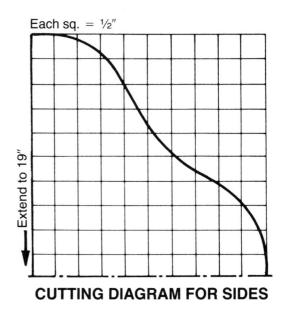

CUTTING DIAGRAM FOR SIDES

Assemble shelves, front strip, partitions, and dividers. Attach drawer partitions to bottom; add side. Add back pieces, nailing into drawer partitions (because they are in line with upper dividers, they can't be nailed on through middle shelf) and into shelves and other dividers.

Glue edging strips on door pieces, following General Directions. Trim doors as required, allowing for hinges. Hinge doors in place. Glue on door stop strips and clamp with spring clothespins until dry. Attach base as shown.

Make drawers to fit spaces with 1/16″ clearance all around, using our dimensions as a guide.

To finish, distress, and then apply stain, following General Directions. When dry, add two coats of polyurethane.

Drill for knobs, and attach as shown.

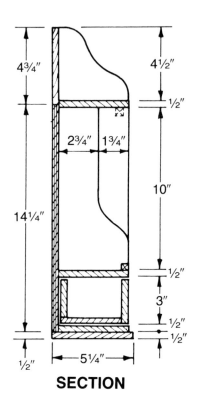

SECTION

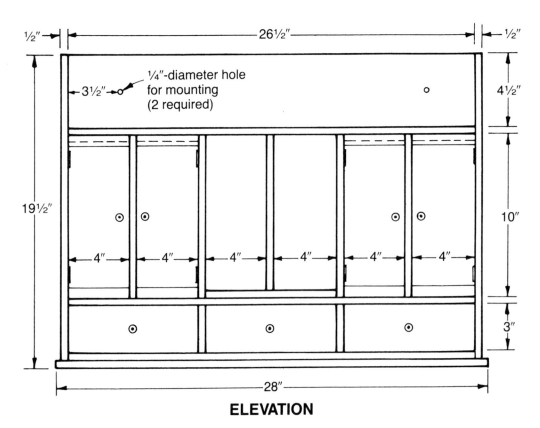

1/4″-diameter hole for mounting (2 required)

ELEVATION

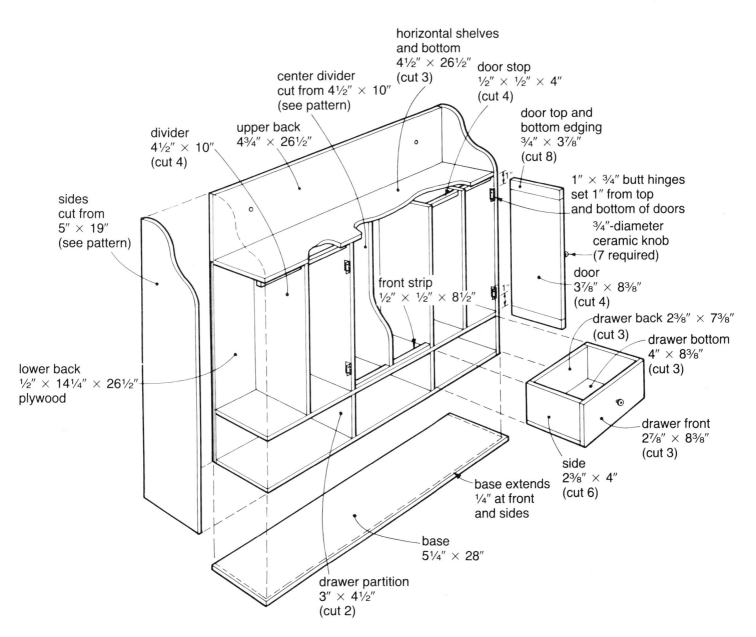

horizontal shelves
and bottom
4½″ × 26½″
(cut 3)

door stop
½″ × ½″ × 4″
(cut 4)

center divider
cut from 4½″ × 10″
(see pattern)

door top and
bottom edging
¾″ × 3⅞″
(cut 8)

upper back
4¾″ × 26½″

divider
4½″ × 10″
(cut 4)

1″ × ¾″ butt hinges
set 1″ from top
and bottom of doors

¾″-diameter
ceramic knob
(7 required)

sides
cut from
5″ × 19″
(see pattern)

front strip
½″ × ½″ × 8½″

door
3⅞″ × 8⅜″
(cut 4)

drawer back 2⅜″ × 7⅜″
(cut 3)

drawer bottom
4″ × 8⅜″
(cut 3)

lower back
½″ × 14¼″ × 26½″
plywood

drawer front
2⅞″ × 8⅜″
(cut 3)

side
2⅜″ × 4″
(cut 6)

base extends
¼″ at front
and sides

base
5¼″ × 28″

drawer partition
3″ × 4½″
(cut 2)

ASSEMBLY DIAGRAM

HEART HANG-UP

Although this is just eight inches across, it's big enough to give you a dramatic background for a small basket or any tiny treasure. Cut pieces from lumber leftovers; wipe on paint for an antique finish.

SIZE:
8¼″ wide × 7¾″ high × 2½″ deep

MATERIALS:
Old scrap ¾″ pine (ours had a crack in it)
White glue
1½″ finishing nails
Artist's acrylic paints: white, black, dark blue, burnt
    umber

TOOLS:
Coping or saber saw, drill, sandpaper

Cut a free-form heart shape 8¼″ wide × 7¾″ high and a curved shelf ¾″ deep × 6½″ wide. Sand slightly but leave edges somewhat rough for "antique" look.

To paint, mix dark blue with a dab of white and black for gray-blue tone. Wipe on, then rub away some paint on lobes of heart to bring out old wood tone. Antique finish, following General Directions.

Glue and nail heart to shelf. Drill ¼″-diameter hole to hang.

COLONIAL
CANDLE
BOX

Keep candles here, right at hand for the times you want their warm glow to mark a special celebration. Or use the box to store pot lids or to show off favorite plants, as in our photograph.

SIZE:
15½″ wide × 8″ high × 5¼″ deep

MATERIALS:
4′ of ½ × 6 pine
2′ of ½ × 8 pine
1¼″ brads
White glue
Pine stain
Polyurethane varnish

TOOLS:
Coping or saber saw, drill, sandpaper

Enlarge pattern for back, following General Directions.
Cut back and then all other parts, following diagrams. Drill
back for hanging holes as shown.

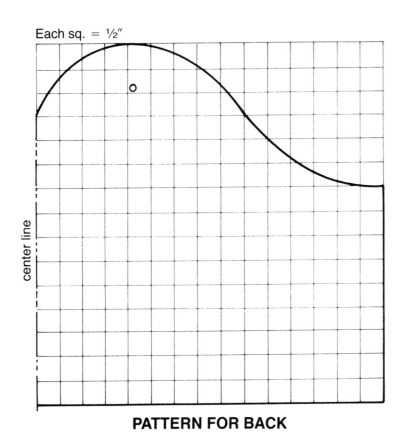

Each sq. = ½"

center line

PATTERN FOR BACK

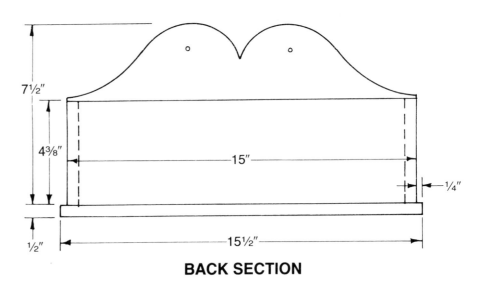

7½"

4⅜"

15"

¼"

½"

15½"

BACK SECTION

Assemble, butting sides between front and back. Then add bottom as shown.

To finish, distress and apply stain, following General Directions. When dry, add two coats of polyurethane.

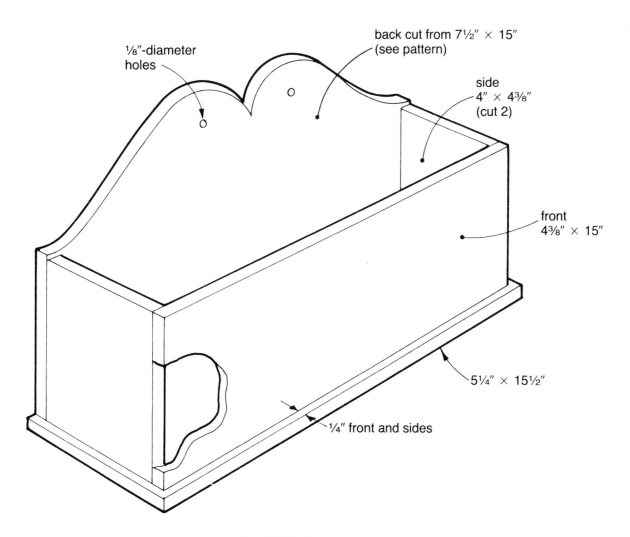

ASSEMBLY DIAGRAM

BARNYARD MUG HOLDER

A good cup of coffee is something to crow over. This barnyard couple may have left their cock-a-doodle-doo behind, but they remembered to bring a set of mugs.

SIZE:
22" wide × 13" high × 6¼" deep

MATERIALS:
2' of 1 × 14 pine for hen, rooster, and eggs
2' of 1 × 6 pine for shelf
1½" No. 8 wood screws
Four 1" cup hooks
Two picture hangers
Artist's acrylic paints: white, black, raw sienna, burnt
     sienna, dark green, red, burnt umber
Polyurethane varnish

TOOLS:
Coping or saber saw

Enlarge patterns, following General Directions. Trace outer edges of hen, rooster, and eggs on pine and cut out.

Paint, using photograph as your color guide. First paint the basecoat colors, raw sienna with touch of white for rooster and gray for hen. Let dry. Then blend colors in rooster tail and ruff and hen's body with fingers or paper towel. Complete details. Paint shelf green. Let dry. Antique all pieces, following General Directions.

Position hen and rooster, then center eggs on back edge of shelf between hen and rooster as shown on pattern, using two screws apiece to fasten each cutout to shelf. Apply polyurethane. Attach cup hooks and picture hangers.

Each sq. = 1"

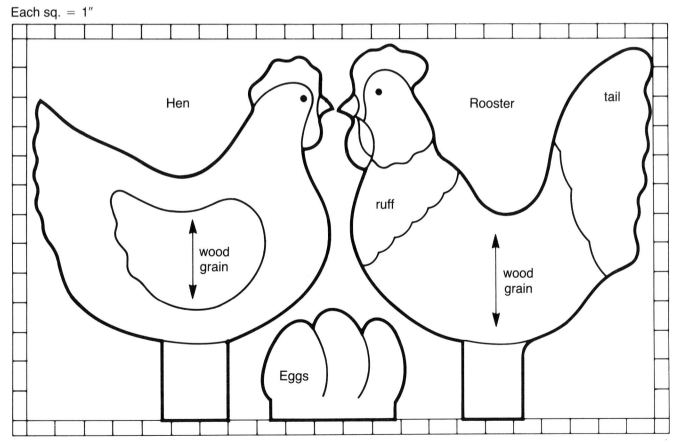

Note: Thin lines represent defined painted areas.

QUAINT COTTAGE

Just the thing for a little child's room! Cut it from plywood and paint it the brightest color you can think of. Then fill its pine ledge with baby's books, crayons, or stuffed animals.

SIZE:
16″ wide × 13¾″ high × 6¼″ deep

MATERIALS:
13¾″ × 16″ piece of ¾″ plywood for house
2′ of 1 × 6 pine for shelf
Two 1′ pieces of 1 × 2 pine for back spacers (not visible in photograph)
1½″ No. 8 wood screws
1¼″ brads
Two screw eyes
Wood filler
Artist's acrylic paints: white, black, red, burnt sienna
Satin polyurethane varnish

TOOLS:
Saber saw, sandpaper, masking tape

Enlarge pattern and trace on plywood, following General Directions; cut out. Fill plywood edges with wood filler; sand smooth.

Center two pine spacers horizontally on back of house about 1½″ from top and bottom edges respectively. Glue and nail.

Use photograph as a guide and paint as follows: Mask roofline. Combine white with a touch of burnt sienna; paint body of house and allow to dry thoroughly. Remove tape and remask roofline on painted side (press tape lightly). Paint roof, chimneys, and shelf burnt sienna mixed with red (about 1 to 1) and a touch of white. Mask areas for windows (teddy bear and doll hide two bottom windows in photograph), doors, and thin vertical line; paint dark gray. Finish with polyurethane.

To assemble, screw through back of house into shelf edge. Attach two screw eyes to top of top spacer. Connect with wire to hang.

Each sq. = 1″

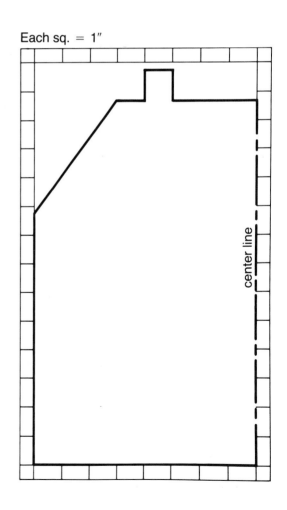

center line

SPICE SPACE

Every kitchen—and every cook—needs a spice rack. This attractive pine version has a nifty top shelf for herb pots or knick-knacks. You can make it to the width specified here or adapt it to the width that best suits you.

SIZE:
17" wide × 15½" high × 3½" deep

MATERIALS:
6' of ½ × 4 pine
1" finishing nails
White glue
Wood filler
Pine stain
Two loop picture hangers

TOOLS:
Saber saw, drill, sandpaper

Following General Directions, enlarge half-pattern for sides (disregard broken line X). Transfer two full patterns to wood; cut out with saber saw. Drill decorative holes. Sand. Cut two 16" shelves.

Mark inside of side pieces 4¾" from top and bottom points for bottom of lower shelf and top of upper shelf.

Start about three nails through sides for shelf until tips just begin to protrude; then glue and nail shelves between sides, wiping away any excess glue. Sink nails; fill holes. Attach hangers at tops of sides. Let dry. Stain.

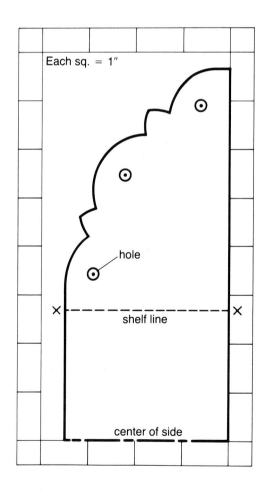

Each sq. = 1"

hole

× shelf line ×

center of side

SHOW-OFF
PLANT
SHELF

*This makes a sturdy base for a
lush, leafy plant.*

SIZE:
8½" wide × 14" high × 7½" deep

MATERIALS:
3' of ½ × 10 pine
1¼" brads
White glue
Pine stain
Polyurethane varnish

TOOLS:
Drill, coping or saber saw

Enlarge patterns, following General Directions. Trace back and sides and cut out. Lay sides on back; measure and cut shelf and front to fit between sides. Test-fit.

Join sides to shelf and front with glue and brads, then sides to back. Stain and finish with polyurethane.

Drill ¼"-diameter hole near top to hang.

Each sq. = 1"

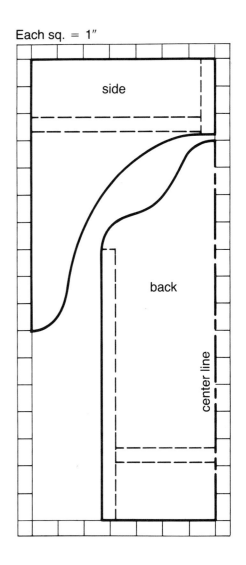

PARTY PLATE RACK

This showcase will display your Sunday china every day of the week.

SIZE:
36" wide × 29¼" high × 8" deep

MATERIALS:
12' of 1 × 10 pine
3' of 1 × 4 pine
3½' of 1 × 6 pine
5' of ½ × 6 pine
6' of ¼" × 1⅜" lattice
Two 8" × 17" pieces of ¼" plywood
9' of ¼" quarter-round molding
White glue
1½" finishing nails
1¼" and ¾" brads
Two 1"-diameter porcelain knobs with screws
Two loop picture hangers
Wood filler
Dark walnut (4 parts) and red mahogany (1 part) stains
Satin polyurethane varnish
Paste wax

TOOLS:
Plane, saber saw, drill, sandpaper, fine steel wool

Enlarge pattern, following General Directions. Trace sides on 1 × 10 and cut out. From remaining 1 × 10, cut two bottom shelves, each 8″ × 34½″, and 8″ × 5¼″ partition for drawers. For top shelf cut 1 × 4 to 34½″. Cut two pieces lattice each 36″.

With glue and 1½″ nails assemble unit, with shelves between sides and partition centered between two bottom shelves. Round edges of lattice with plane or sandpaper. Glue and nail to sides, as shown, with ¾″ brads.

For drawers, construct open-top boxes as follows: Use 1 × 6 pine for fronts; ½ × 6 pine for sides and backs, and plywood for bottoms. Allow a ¹⁄₁₆″ space between drawer and opening.

Nail bottoms to sides and back, then front to sides, keeping plywood flush with bottom edge of front. Glue strips of quarter-round on inside to support bottom at front. Cut and glue remaining quarter-round on shelves, 1½″ from back, for plate stop (not shown). Sink nails and fill holes.

Stain, following General Directions. Use steel wool instead of sandpaper in between coats. (See General Directions for staining to achieve this fine finish.) When dry, finish with polyurethane; let dry. Apply a coat of paste wax. Drill holes for knobs through center of drawer fronts and screw knobs in place. Attach picture hangers near top back edge of sides.

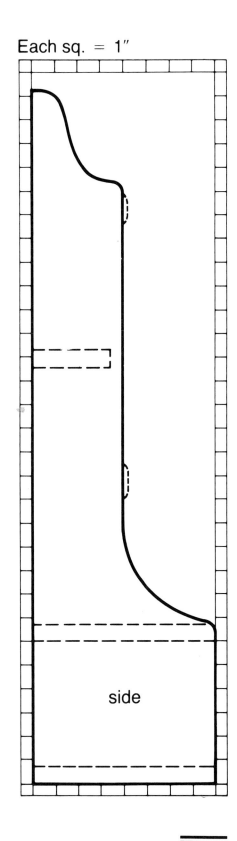

Each sq. = 1″

side

CHIEF CHEF
FOR HERB AND
SPICE FANCIERS

This small hang-up designed in Shaker style is a wonder at saving space. Its top shelf makes a perfect home for your tallest pepper mill.

Enlarge patterns, following General Directions; trace back and sides on pine; cut out.

Test-fit back, and cut shelves to fit between sides. Sand edges smooth. Assemble with glue and nails. Set nails and fill holes with wood filler. Stain and finish with polyurethane and paste wax. Attach hangers.

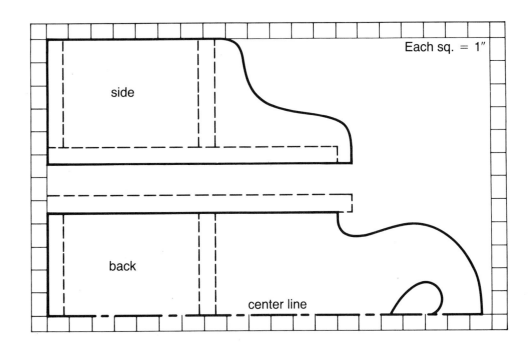

COZY CORNER WHATNOT SHELF

Here's a first-rate candidate for that corner you thought you'd never fill. Its three shelves of graduated size give you a chance to display an assortment of your small treasures.

SIZE:
33" high

MATERIALS:
8' of ½ × 10 pine
White glue
Brads
Pine stain
Artist's acrylic paint: burnt umber
Polyurethane varnish
Paste wax
Two sawtooth hangers

TOOLS
Coping or saber saw, sandpaper, rag, compass

Enlarge pattern, following General Directions, then cut two sides from ½" pine, cutting one to broken line.

Mark for shelves. Cut shelves to quarter-round shape, using compass to mark desired arc.

Glue and nail sides together; add shelves. Apply antique pine finish, following General Directions. Attach hangers.

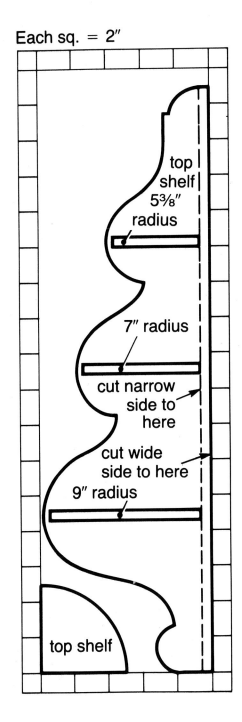

Each sq. = 2"

top shelf 5⅜" radius

7" radius

cut narrow side to here

cut wide side to here

9" radius

top shelf

WOODSY
WALL
SCONCE

Set out a pretty decorative candle or a leafy potted plant on this sturdy wall sconce.

SIZE:
6¼" wide × 14" high × 4½" deep

MATERIALS:
4' of ½ × 8 pine
White glue
Artist's acrylic paint: burnt umber
Pine stain
Paste wax

TOOLS:
Drill, coping or saber saw

Enlarge pattern and transfer to wood, following General Directions.

Cut both sides at once by temporarily nailing two pieces of wood together. Cut bottom and back, rounding edges as in diagram. Drill hole in back; glue and nail pieces together.

Apply antique pine finish, following General Directions.

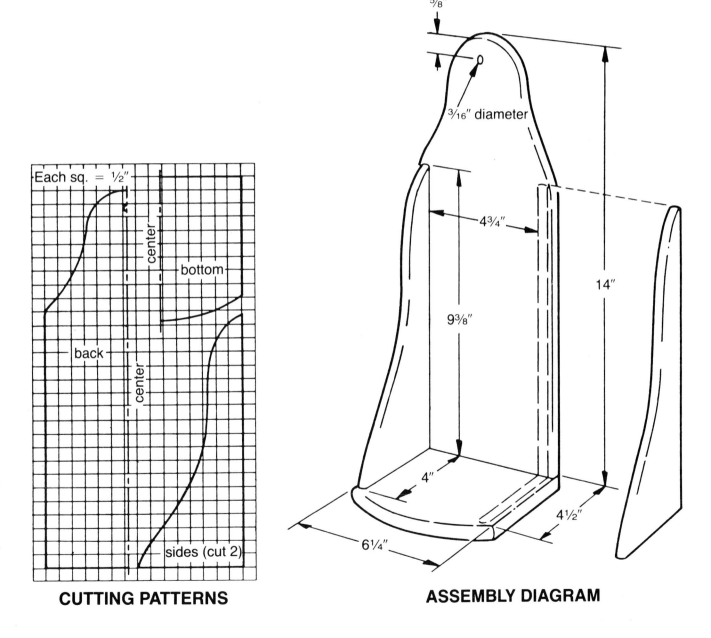

Each sq. = ½"

center

bottom

back

center

sides (cut 2)

CUTTING PATTERNS

⅝"

³⁄₁₆" diameter

4¾"

9⅜"

14"

4"

4½"

6¼"

ASSEMBLY DIAGRAM

OLD-TIME PICTURE FRAME

Any one can look like a pioneer in this rustic hand-made frame. All it takes is four pieces of pine glued together, then cut to shape.

SIZE:
8″ diameter

MATERIALS:
2′ of ½ × 6 pine
One 1″ brass ring pull
Double-thick glass
White glue
Brads
Pine stain
Artist's acrylic paint: burnt umber
Cardboard
Paste wax

TOOLS:
Coping or saber saw, miter box, sandpaper, clamp, drill, steel wool

Enlarge pattern, following General Directions. Cut four 2″ × 8″ pieces; miter ends at a 45° angle and cut a ¼″ × ¼″ rabbet in each. Glue and clamp pieces together to make a square frame, following photograph for grain of wood.

Cut frame into a circle with a 4″ radius as in diagram, and drill for ring pull. Round edges and sand surfaces well. Apply antique pine finish, following General Directions, and attach pull.

Cut glass into a 4½″ square and place into rabbet. Add picture and attach cardboard behind with brads.

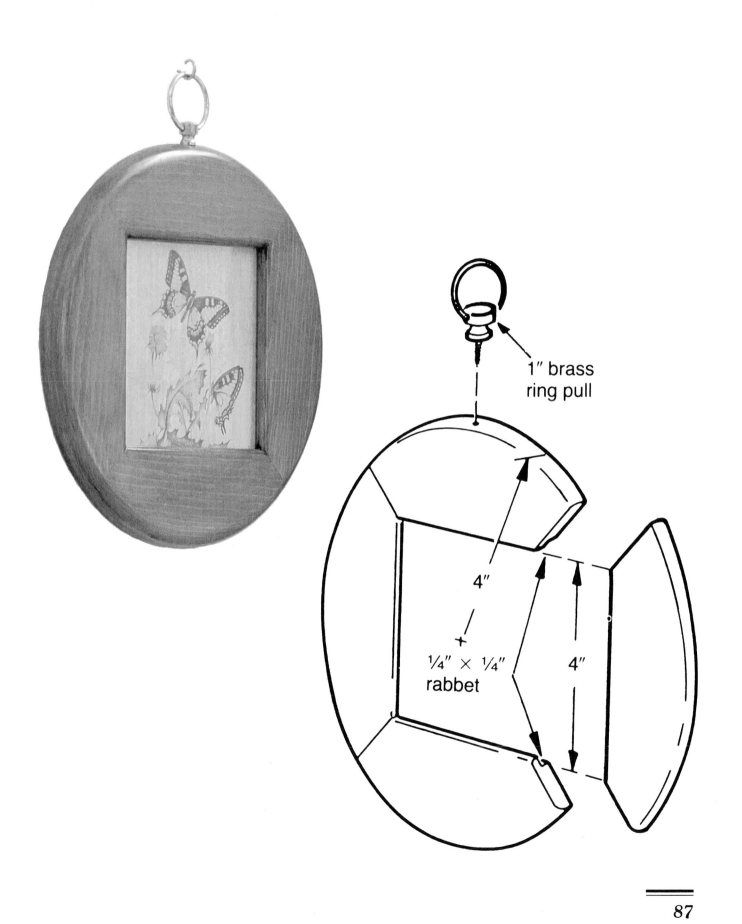

1″ brass
ring pull

4″

+

¼″ × ¼″
rabbet

4″

WATERMELON
BOOKSHELF

Use this tasteful melon to hold the book or two you find you use the most. That might be a recipe collection, your address book, or a diary, if you keep one.

SIZE:
21¼″ wide × 5″ high × 4½″ deep

MATERIALS:
3′ of 1 × 6 pine
1½″ No. 8 wood screws
Two loop picture hangers
Artist's acrylic paints: red, dark green, black, burnt umber
Polyurethane varnish

TOOLS:
Coping or saber saw, plane (optional), sandpaper, compass

Cut shelf 4½″ × 21¼″; round front edge with sandpaper or plane. For watermelon brackets, use a compass to mark quarter-circles with 4″ radius; cut out.

Paint shelf and brackets, using photograph as guide. Antique pieces (see General Directions).

Position brackets 3″ from each end and screw in place. Apply polyurethane. Attach hangers at top of brackets.

COUNTRY
WELCOMERS

Here are a baker's dozen ways to make the outside of your home as inviting as the inside. Greet your guests with just a few of these glorious country-style ornaments. It's the traditional American way to say a friendly hello.

"I LOVE AMERICA" HEART

This emblem will brighten up that space under the eaves, on a garden gate, or even on the old oak tree. The pine heart has stenciled stars and red lattice stripes.

SIZE:
14″ wide × 15″ high

MATERIALS:
14″ × 15″ piece of ½″ plywood
4′ of 1⅛″ × ¼″ lattice
Waterproof glue
Exterior primer
Artist's acrylic paints: red, white, and blue
Self-adhesive vinyl
Polyurethane varnish

TOOLS:
Coping or saber saw, sandpaper

Enlarge pattern and transfer design to wood, following General Directions.

Cut out heart and lattice strips. Prime heart and strips. Sand smooth. With stencil, blot out stars, following General Directions, and paint blue background. Remove stencils.

Paint lattice strips red. When dry, glue on. Finish with two coats polyurethane.

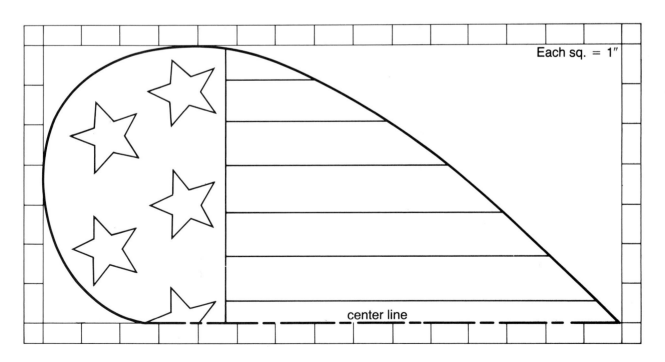

Each sq. = 1″

center line

WONDERFUL WELCOME

Tack this inviting sign on the front door or gate. The stenciled design sends the message in pictures, and the letters make sure no one can mistake it.

SIZE:
12½″ wide × 8″ high

MATERIALS:
12″ × 18″ piece of ½″ plywood
Exterior primer
Artist's acrylic paints: barn red, cream, beige, light blue,
    dark brown or black
Polyurethane varnish
Purchased alphabet stencils
Self-adhesive vinyl

TOOLS:
Coping or saber saw, sandpaper, pointed brush, carbon
paper, stencil brush, craft knife

Enlarge pattern and transfer outline to wood, following General Directions. Cut out and sand smooth, carefully rounding edges. Prime and sand. Following photograph for color, paint background.

Transfer leaf motifs, cuffs, and hands to self-adhesive vinyl, and cut out. Stencil leaf motifs, cuffs, hands (not finger details), and lettering, following General Directions. Shade lower edge of sleeves. Transfer finger outlines and paint with pointed brush, shading edges. When dry, apply two coats of polyurethane to front and back.

Each sq. = 1″

AUTUMN ACORN SHUTTER TRIM

Customize your shutters with this acorn and oak-leaf pattern. Even an all-thumbs artist will find the painted brushwork simple with our diagram.

SIZE:
16" wide × 6" high

MATERIALS:
16" × 7" piece of ½" plywood
Exterior primer
Artist's acrylic paints: mustard, cream, burnt umber, dark
     green, olive green
Self-adhesive vinyl
Exterior caulk
Polyurethane varnish

TOOLS:
Sponge and brush, craft knife, coping or saber saw, sandpaper, carbon paper, stencil brush

Enlarge pattern and transfer outline to wood, following General Directions. Cut out and sand smooth, carefully rounding edges. Prime and sand. Following photograph for color, paint background.

Transfer leaf and acorn stencil designs to self-adhesive vinyl and cut out. Stencil leaf on plaque, following General Directions; then add acorn. Stencil leaf veins over leaves. When dry, apply two coats of polyurethane to front and back. Exterior caulk can be used to attach plaque to shutter.

Each sq. = 1″

THREE
BACKYARD
CRITTERS

Delightful animal friends that won't scamper away, get into your garbage, or ravage your cabbage patch. They'll lend an amusing touch to any garden walk and will enchant all the small fry in the neighborhood.

WHIMSICAL
SQUIRREL

SIZE:
Approximately 12″ wide × 6″ high

MATERIALS:
½″ plywood 1″ larger all around than finished
    measurement
Exterior primer
Artist's acrylic paints: gold, brick, barn red
Polyurethane varnish
Dowel (optional)

TOOLS:
Coping saw, drill (optional), carbon paper, sandpaper

Enlarge pattern and transfer outline to wood, following General Directions. Cut out. Sand smooth and round edges. Apply a coat of primer and sand again.

With carbon paper, transfer body details onto piece. Following photograph for color, paint squirrel details.

Attach a wood triangle to stand the squirrel on porch, or drill a hole in edge and insert a short dowel to set piece in garden. Finish with two coats of polyurethane on front and back.

Each sq. = 1″

FRISKY
RACCOON

SIZE:
Approximately 16″ wide × 9″ high

MATERIALS:
½″ plywood 1″ larger around than finished measurement
Exterior primer
Artist's acrylic paints: barn red, raw sienna, soft black, mustard, off-white
Polyurethane varnish
Dowel (optional)

TOOLS:
Coping saw, drill (optional), carbon paper, sandpaper

Enlarge pattern and transfer to wood, following General Directions. Cut out. Sand smooth and round edges. Apply a coat of primer and sand again.

With carbon paper, transfer body details onto piece. Following photograph for color, paint raccoon details.

Attach a wood triangle to stand raccoon on porch, or drill a hole in edge and insert a short dowel to set piece in garden. Finish with two coats of polyurethane on front and back.

Each sq. = 1″

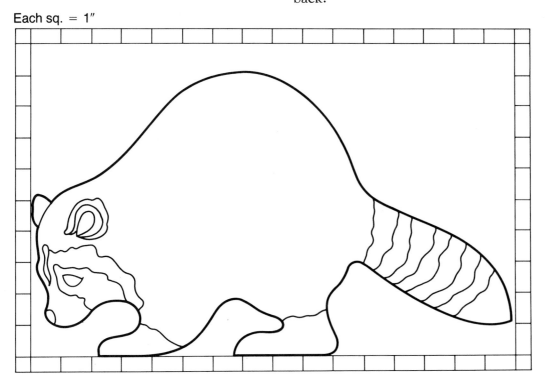

FRIENDLY BUNNY

Each sq. = 1″

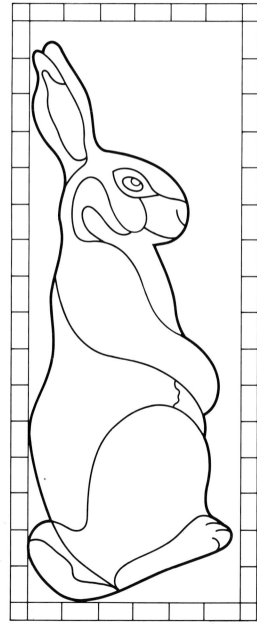

SIZE:
Approximately 7″ wide × 14¾″ high

MATERIALS:
½″ plywood 1″ larger all around than finished
    measurement
Exterior primer
Artist's acrylic paints: raw sienna, off-white, soft black,
    burnt umber
Polyurethane varnish

TOOLS:
Coping saw, drill (optional), carbon paper, sandpaper

Enlarge pattern and transfer outline to wood, following General Directions. Cut out. Sand smooth and round edges. Apply a coat of primer and sand again.

With carbon paper, transfer body details onto piece. Paint bunny, using photograph as color guide.

Attach a wood triangle to stand bunny on porch, or drill a hole in edge and insert a short dowel to set piece in garden. Finish with two coats of polyurethane on front and back.

PURRS
FOR THE
POSTMAN

*Here's a pair of handsome
calico kitties that anyone would
love to have around. You can
paint them with the markings of
your own pet or the tom that
lives down the street.*

SIZE:
15½" wide × 11½" high

MATERIALS:
1½' × 2' piece of ½" plywood
Exterior primer
Artist's acrylic paints: gold, brick red, raw sienna, black,
    off-white, gray
Polyurethane varnish
Exterior adhesive caulk

TOOLS:
Coping saw, carbon paper, sandpaper

Enlarge pattern and transfer outlines to wood, following General Directions. Make two, one reversed. Cut out and sand smooth. Apply coat of primer and sand again.

Transfer details with carbon paper. Paint details following photograph for color. When dry, rub on coat of thinned raw sienna for antique look (see General Directions).

Finish with two coats of polyurethane on front and back. Attach kitties to mailbox with exterior adhesive caulk or screws.

Each sq. = 1"

PRETTY PLANTER

Here's a project where half the work is already done. Decorate a half-barrel planter from the nursery or garden center with stenciled border patterns. Muted paint colors look especially good on the wood, and your end result makes a fine bed for any flowering plant.

MATERIALS:
Half-barrel (from lumberyard or nursery)
Artist's acrylic paints: red, blue, olive green
Self-adhesive vinyl

TOOLS:
Sponge or brush, craft knife, stencil brush

Enlarge design, following General Directions. Transfer to self-adhesive vinyl, and cut out. Stencil, following General Directions.

Each sq. = 2"

COCK-OF-THE-WALK

This garden rooster is cut from rough lumber that weathers after a few weeks to a lovely barn gray. If you're in a hurry, you can use a driftwood stain for the same effect.

SIZE:
24" wide × 13" high (without rod)

MATERIALS:
4½' of 1 × 8 No. 2 pine or rough-cut cedar, if available
Waterproof wood glue
½" × 14" threaded metal rod
Nut and washer
Two ½" flathead nails
Driftwood stain (optional)

TOOLS:
Coping saw, drill with ½" spade or shovel bit, clamps, sandpaper

Use waterproof glue to join the pine or rough-cut cedar to accommodate rooster pattern; sand matched edges smooth. Enlarge pattern and transfer to wood, following General Directions.

Cut out rooster. Then, with ½"-diameter spade or shovel bit, drill hole between dotted lines for ½" × 14" threaded metal rod. Insert rod, place nut and washer above and below rooster. Hammer short flathead nail in each side for eyes.

Do not apply protective coating. Let rooster weather outdoors, or stain with driftwood stain.

Each sq. = 2"

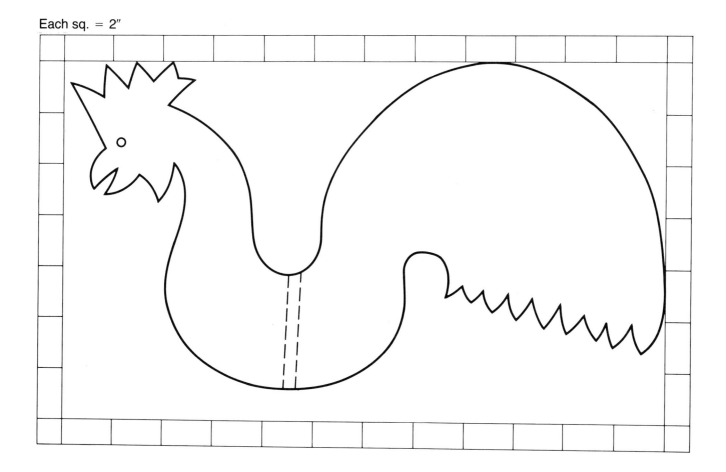

COUNTRY
LANDSCAPE

*Paint this bit of nostalgia on a
long board to span a lintel of
any front door, set of garage
doors, or wide window. Our
clear pattern makes it all easy.*

SIZE:
30″ wide × 4½″ high

MATERIALS:
3′ of 1 × 6 pine
Exterior primer
Artist's acrylic paints: gold, black, mustard, off-white,
    red, light pink, blue, dark green, light green
Self-adhesive vinyl
Polyurethane varnish

TOOLS:
Coping or saber saw, stencil brushes, craft knife

Enlarge and transfer curved outline to wood, following General Directions. Cut out.

Enlarge country scene and transfer to self-adhesive vinyl, and to the wood. Cut around shapes (house, trees, animals, etc.) on the vinyl, and peel away background. Use shapes remaining to block out figures on the wood.

Paint sky and grass, going right over shapes and letting wood grain show for stained look. Let dry.

Remove vinyl and paint figures and house; let dry. Then stencil windows over house. Shade edges of trees and bushes with dry brush dipped in deep forest green; let dry; go over inside of bushes with same green mixed with blue. Paint apples on trees. When dry, finish with two coats of polyurethane on back and front.

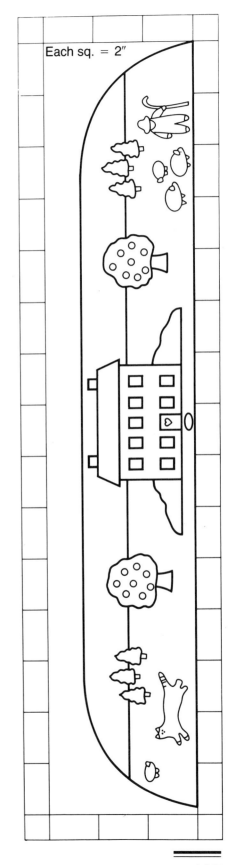

Each sq. = 2″

BLOOMING HOSE HOLDER

Make a splash with this colorful wooden garden, chock-full of painted tulips. These flowers are guaranteed to bloom in all seasons.

SIZE:
19" wide × 9" high × 6¼" deep

MATERIALS:
20" × 30" piece of ½" exterior-grade plywood
1½" screws
Galvanized nails
Artist's acrylic paints: red, gray, pale green, dark green
Wood filler
Sawtooth hanger

TOOLS:
Saber saw

From plywood, cut back, 14″ × 9″; shelf, 6¼″ × 14″; shelf front, 3¼″ × 14″.

Enlarge tulip pattern, following General Directions. Transfer design to wood by centering pattern on upper part of back piece. Cut out, leaving lower 5¼″ section to run full width of wood. Fill edges around outside.

Screw shelf to lower edge of back; nail front to front edge of shelf. Paint tulip pattern directly on unprimed wood for stained look; paint remaining sections gray.

Fasten to wall by screwing through back.

Each sq. = 1″

center line

PINEAPPLE NAMEPLATE

The pineapple was a colonial symbol of welcome. Tag one onto your gate with your stenciled nameplate below for your own personal welcome mat.

SIZE:
11″ wide × 15½″ high

MATERIALS:
12″ × 16″ piece of ½″ exterior-grade plywood
Exterior primer
Artist's acrylic paints: light green, raw sienna, gold, mustard, red, dark green
Wood filler
Self-adhesive vinyl
Polyurethane varnish
Purchased alphabet stencils
Sawtooth hanger

TOOLS:
Coping saw, brushes, sandpaper, stencil brush

Enlarge pattern and transfer design to wood, following General Directions. Cut out. Fill plywood edges and sand smooth, rounding edges. Prime.

Paint entire pineapple gold, scroll mustard, and leaves dark green. When dry, block out lattice work on pineapple and inner leaves with self-adhesive vinyl; paint outer edge of leaves, "diamonds" on pineapple, and stencil lettering on scroll. When dry, finish with two coats of polyurethane on front and back.

Attach sawtooth hanger.

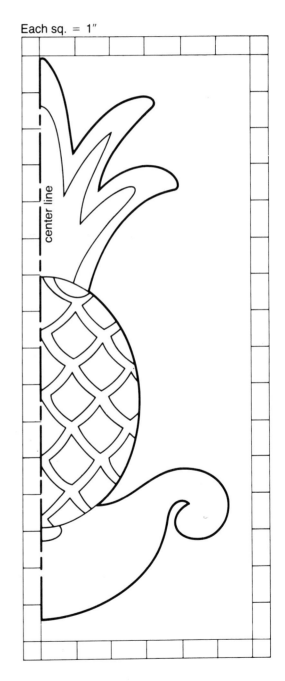

Each sq. = 1″

center line

GOSSIPING
GEESE

Children will love this pair of gossiping geese. Cut them out of pine, paint, then mount on dowels.

Enlarge patterns and transfer to wood, following General Directions. Cut out geese and raised wings separately. Fill edges.

With sander, bevel inner surface of lower part of wings so that they stand away from body at an angle. Drill ½″-deep hole in edge at X for dowel.

Each sq. = 2″

Paint both sides of geese and wings, as in pattern; glue and tack wings in place, sinking nails and filling holes. Let dry, and touch up holes. Rub a watery coat of gray over back and wings, raw umber over belly; wipe off immediately to antique surface.

Paint dowel black, leaving top ½″ unpainted. Insert dowel, gluing to hold.

Each sq. = 1″

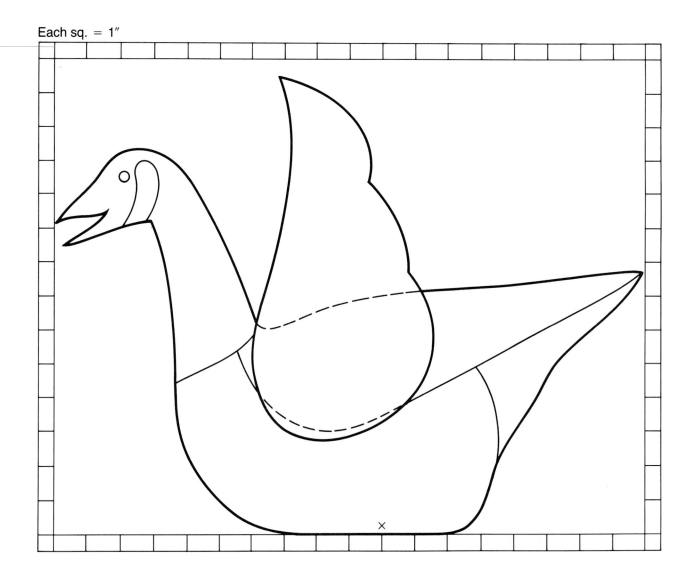

SOMETHING SPECIAL FOR SOMEBODY SPECIAL

We hope the items in this book will tempt you to make something special for someone dear to you—someone who would always cherish a gift that expresses your investment of time and talent and love.

In this chapter we show some extra-special projects—for the children in your family, close friends, or favorite relatives.

PICKET FENCE PLATE RACK

If you like collectibles, keepsakes, or just pretty dishes, you will love this picket fence plate rack. With very few vertical and horizontal pieces of wood, it creates a perfect showcase for your favorite things.

SIZE:
40½" wide × 37¼" high × 6¼" deep

MATERIALS:
32' of ½ × 3 pine
16' of 1 × 8 pine
8' of 1 × 6 pine
8' of ⅜"-diameter quarter-round molding
1¼" finishing nails
1" and ½" brads
Hollow-wall fasteners
White glue
Fruitwood stain
Polyurethane varnish

TOOLS:
Saber saw, drill, sandpaper

From ½ × 3 pine, cut eleven vertical slats, each 30" long. From 1 × 8 pine, cut two sides, 37¼" long; crown, 39" long; and top shelf, 6" × 39". From 1 × 6 pine, cut middle and bottom shelves, 5½" × 39". Following General Directions, enlarge patterns for sides and crown. Trace, then cut. Sand all edges smooth.

Cut two pieces of 39" molding and use glue and ½" brads to attach to one long edge of middle and bottom shelves. Wipe away excess glue. To assemble: mark placement of top, middle, and bottom shelves on both sides of side pieces. (Bottom and middle shelves are recessed ½" from back edges to receive slats.) Assemble shelves between sides with glue and finishing nails. (*Hint:* Drive nails into sides until almost through, then drive into joining piece.)

To attach slats, lay unit facedown on flat surface and evenly space slats approximately 1⅛" apart, with end slats butting against sides. Apply glue to edges of shelves where slats will go, as well as to tops of slats, then nail in place using 1" brads to go through slats and 1¼" nails to go through top shelf into slats.

Glue and nail crown to sides and top shelf. (*Hint:* Turn unit upside down; drive a few nails through top shelf into crown.) Stain and, when dry, apply polyurethane. To hang, drill clearance holes for fasteners through two slats or through crown.

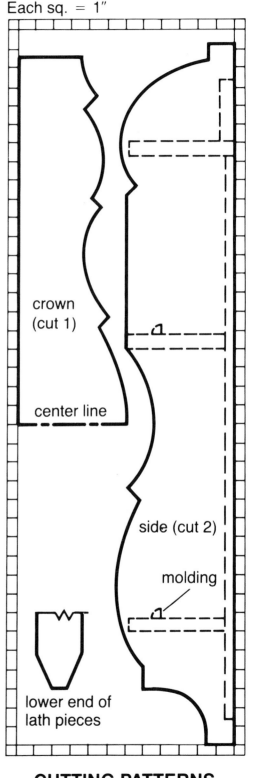

Each sq. = 1"

crown (cut 1)

center line

side (cut 2)

molding

lower end of lath pieces

CUTTING PATTERNS

HEART ROCKER

This darling rocker will win the heart of any little girl or boy. Just cut out four shapes with a saber saw, then finish with polyurethane oil or pine stain.

From 1 × 12 wood, cut the following: back, 11½″ × 27″; two upper sides, 11½″ × 18½″; two lower sides, 7″ × 27″; seat, 10½″ × 11½″; front apron, 2¾″ × 11½″; two cleats, 2″ × 9″.

Enlarge patterns, following General Directions, and transfer to wood; cut out. Also cut out heart shape, following General Directions.

Glue upper and lower sides together as shown in assembly diagram. Then center, glue, and screw cleat over joint on inside of side pieces. Since this will act as a seat support, cleats must line up accurately with each other. Sand joints smooth.

Predrill holes for screws with three-in-one drill bit, sinking heads ¼″. Glue and screw apron to bottom of seat, about ¾″ from front. Glue and screw back to seat, and then sides to seat and back. Screw seat to cleats from underneath. Glue in wood plugs to fill all screw holes; sand flush.

Apply two or three coats of polyurethane oil, sanding lightly between coats, or stain.

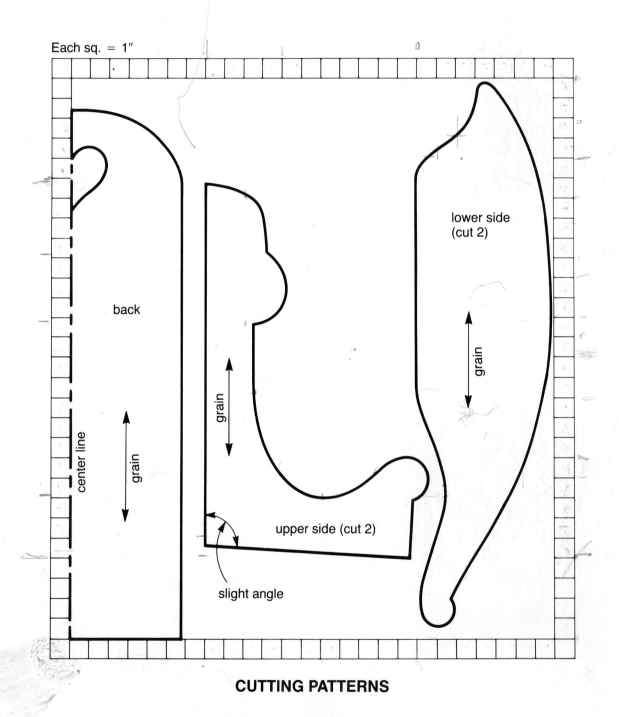

Each sq. = 1"

back

center line

grain

grain

slight angle

upper side (cut 2)

lower side
(cut 2)

grain

grain

CUTTING PATTERNS

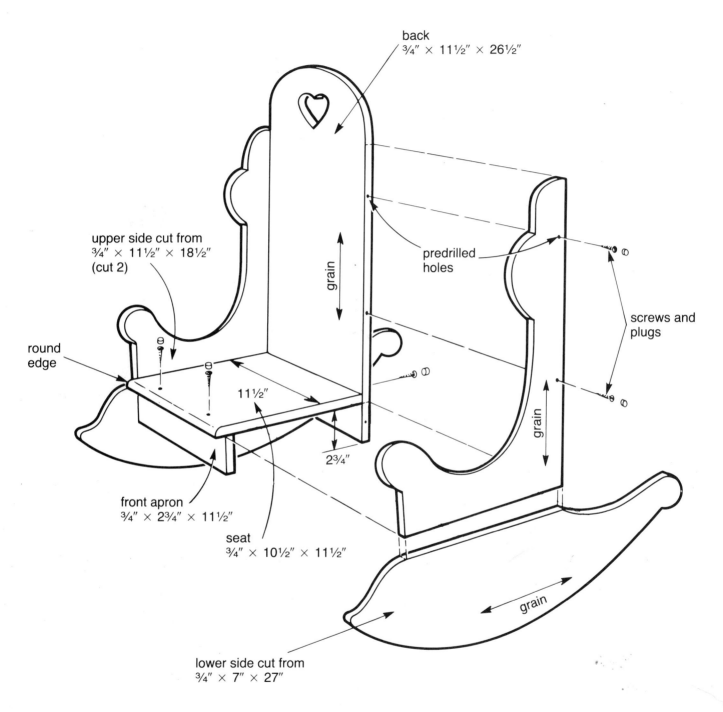

back
¾" × 11½" × 26½"

upper side cut from
¾" × 11½" × 18½"
(cut 2)

predrilled
holes

grain

screws and
plugs

round
edge

grain

11½"

2¾"

front apron
¾" × 2¾" × 11½"

seat
¾" × 10½" × 11½"

grain

lower side cut from
¾" × 7" × 27"

ASSEMBLY DIAGRAM

HAPPY BABY
LOW CHAIR

Here's a loving gift for a very lucky tot. The low chair puts her closer to mom and dad and cuts the risk of high-rise falls. A durable polyurethane finish protects the wood, and the tray pulls out for easy access.

From 1 × 12, cut the following: back, 11¼" × 23"; two sides, 11" × 11"; seat, 9" × 11¼"; tray, 7½" ×s 15½·.

Enlarge pattern for back, following General Directions, and transfer to pine; cut out. For tapered curve along front edge of sides, mark 10" width at midpoint, then draw tapered curve. Using back pattern, transfer curve of arc, centering it along bottom edge of sides.

Clamp sides together, trim front, and cut out arc. Round all cut edges with rasp and sandpaper. Test-assemble back between sides, making certain sides are square. Glue and nail back and seat between sides.

From remaining pine, cut slide tray. Round front corners and mark cutout indentation along back edge as indicated. Sand smooth, rounding all edges. Cut 7½"-long tray slides from 1 × 1 pine; sand, glue, and screw to sides. Construct two L-shaped tray brackets, as shown, by screwing 5" piece of 1 × 1 at right angles to a 5" piece of 1 × 2. Attach with glue and screws to underside of tray flush with back and side edges.

Set nails. Countersink screws. Fill and sand smooth. Apply several coats of polyurethane, sanding lightly between coats.

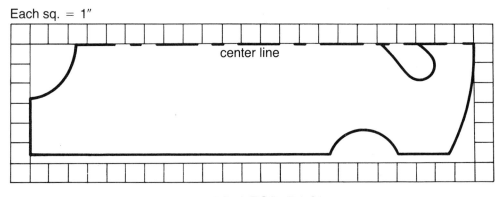

Each sq. = 1"

center line

PATTERN FOR BACK

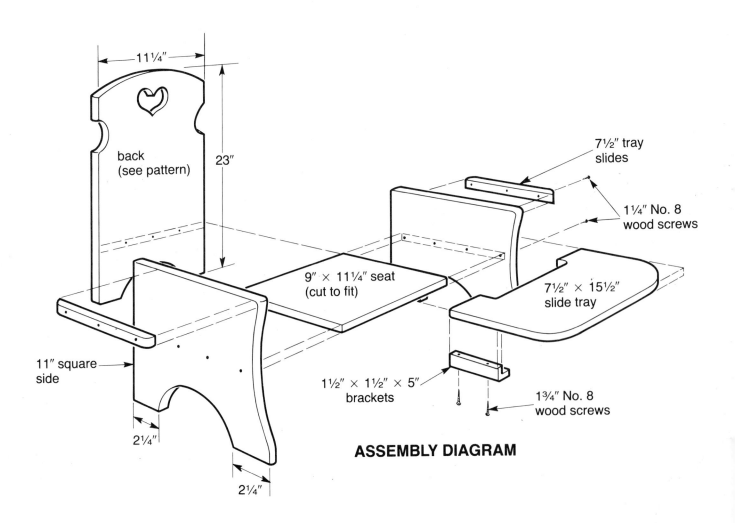

11¼"

back
(see pattern)

23"

7½" tray
slides

1¼" No. 8
wood screws

9" × 11¼" seat
(cut to fit)

7½" × 15½"
slide tray

11" square
side

1½" × 1½" × 5"
brackets

1¾" No. 8
wood screws

2¼"

2¼"

ASSEMBLY DIAGRAM

VERSATILE
SPOON
RACK

Spoons were treasured items in colonial homes, and here's a charming way to showcase— and keep track of—your own. The rack can be adapted for any collection you want to display, and the shelf can be used for bric-a-brac as well as dried flowers or potted plants.

SIZE:
15½" wide × 24" high × 5¼" deep

MATERIALS:
4' of 1 × 10 pine for back
3' of ½ × 6 pine
White glue
1½" brads
¾" escutcheon pins
Pine stain
Low-luster polyurethane varnish
Paste wax

TOOLS:
Coping saw, saber saw, drill, plane, sandpaper

Referring to General Directions for joining boards for wider widths, cut two 2' pine lengths and join for shaped display rack back. Following General Directions, enlarge pattern for back, trace on pine, and cut out. From ½ × 6 pine cut bottom of planter box to size, as indicated on the assembly diagram.

Enlarge and transfer patterns for the planter box sides, front, and bracket on remaining ½ × 6 pine; cut out. Also, cut out one spoon holder and check a spoon in holder for fit. Adjust if necessary and cut out a total of six holders. On back piece, mark and drill ¼"-diameter hole to hang display rack; then mark placement for spoon holders.

Following the assembly diagram, glue and nail planter box sides to front with top and side edges flush. Use plane to bevel lower edges of front and sides to 15° angle until they fit flush against bottom of planter box section.

Attach bottom flush with back edges of sides, extending ¼" at front and ½" at each side. Mark placement for planter box on back, 19¼" from top and centered; attach with glue and 1½" brads. Glue and nail bracket to center of bottom and to back as shown. Use ¾" escutcheon pins to attach spoon holders from front.

Sand, round all edges, and distress. Apply finish, following General Directions.

Each sq. = ½″

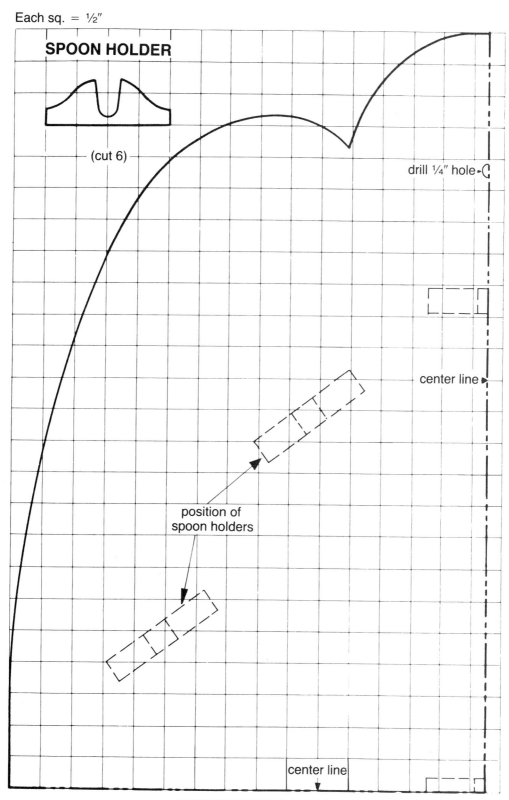

SPOON HOLDER

(cut 6)

drill ¼″ hole

center line

position of
spoon holders

center line

PATTERN FOR BACK

Each sq. = ½″

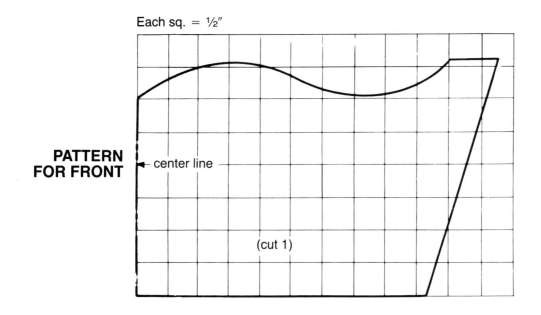

PATTERN FOR FRONT ← center line

(cut 1)

Each sq. = ½″

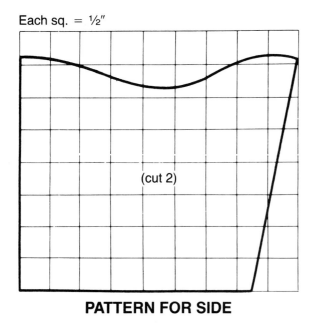

(cut 2)

PATTERN FOR SIDE

Each sq. = ½″

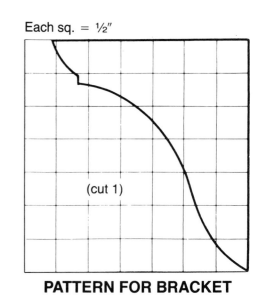

(cut 1)

PATTERN FOR BRACKET

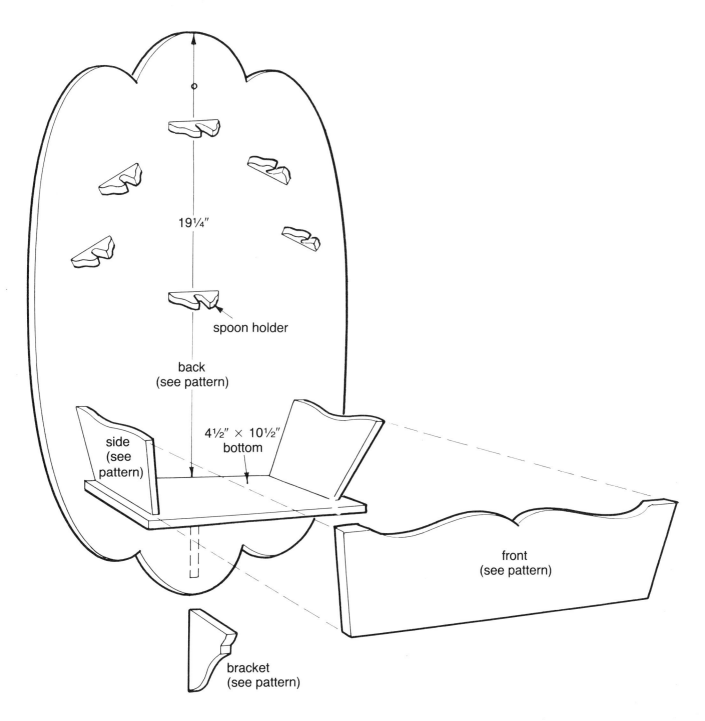

19¼"

spoon holder

back
(see pattern)

side
(see
pattern)

4½" × 10½"
bottom

front
(see pattern)

bracket
(see pattern)

ASSEMBLY DIAGRAM

ROCK-A-BYE DOLL CRADLE

What little girl could resist this darling doll cradle? She will surely cherish it enough to save it for her own little girl. Constructed of half-inch pine shaped with a saber saw, it is finished with stain and polyurethane—and not at all difficult to make.

SIZE:
15" long × 9½" high × 11" wide

MATERIALS:
7' of ½ × 10 pine
3' of 1 × 1 pine
¼" wood plugs
1" No. 6 screws
Fruitwood stain
Polyurethane varnish

TOOLS:
Saber saw, drill, rasp, sandpaper

From ½ × 10 pine, cut the following: headboard, 8″ × 8″; footboard, 5½″ × 7″; two sides, 7″ × 14″; two rockers, 1½″ × 11″.

Enlarge patterns, following General Directions. Transfer to ½ × 10 pine and cut out.

Cut two 6½″ and two 9″ corner posts from 1 × 1 (actually ¾″ × ¾″) pine. Glue and screw posts first to side edges of headboard and footboard, making sure posts extend 1″ above and 1″ below and are flush with inside surfaces.

Countersink screwheads in ¼″-diameter × ¼″-deep hole. Plug screw holes with wood plugs. Attach sides to head and foot in same fashion.

Screw rockers against posts (but do not countersink screwheads as deep as others) and plug, leaving ⅜″ space between bottom of cradle and top edge of rocker (see photograph). Cut bottom to fit inside cradle; glue. Sand, rounding corners of posts. Stain and finish, following General Directions.

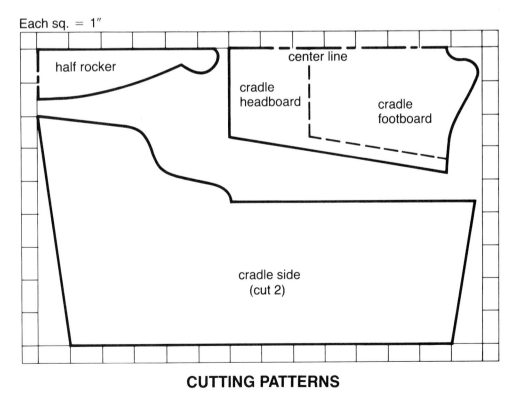

Each sq. = 1″

half rocker

center line

cradle headboard

cradle footboard

cradle side (cut 2)

CUTTING PATTERNS

SWEET BOX FOR VALENTINES

Use this old-time salt box for storing letters, string, coupons—all those odds and ends you want to put away, but not too far.

SIZE:
11″ wide × 16¼″ high × 6¼″ deep

MATERIALS:
8′ of ½ × 10 pine
2′ of ¼″ × 1⅜″ lattice
1 square foot of ⅛″ plywood or hardboard
One ¾″-diameter knob with screw
One ⁷⁄₁₆″ wood plug
One pair of ¾″ × 1″ hinges with screws
1¼″ brads
White glue
Pine stain
Polyurethane varnish

TOOLS:
Coping and saber saw with fine blade, drill with ⁷⁄₁₆″
counterbore bit, sandpaper

From ½ × 10 pine, cut the following: two sides, 5¾″ ×
10″; back, 9½″ × 16¼″; front, 7¼″ × 10½″; lid center
panel, 7″ × 9½″; two lid ends, ¾″ × 7″; two bottoms,
5¼″ × 9½″; drawer front and back, 1¼″ × 7½″; false
drawer front, 2″ × 9″.

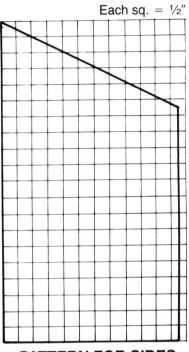

Each sq. = ½″

PATTERN FOR SIDES

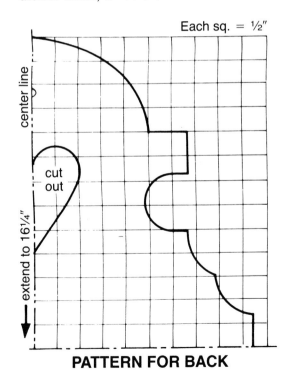

Each sq. = ½″

center line

extend to 16¼″

cut out

PATTERN FOR BACK

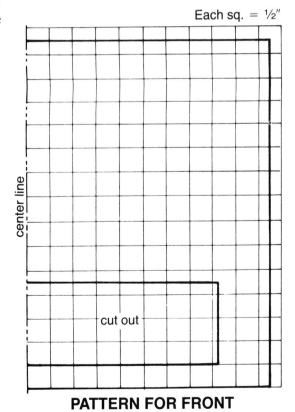

Each sq. = ½″

center line

cut out

PATTERN FOR FRONT

From lattice, cut two drawer sides, 1¼″ × 5¾″; drawer divider, 1¼″ × 4¾″.

Following General Directions and cutting diagrams, enlarge patterns for back and sides. Trace on wood, then cut. Drill starter holes for heart and drawer, following General Directions. Insert blade and cut out. Use counterbore bit to drill hole for nail and plug to hang.

Attach edging strips to lid, following General Directions.

Assemble four sides around bottom and inside shelf. Make drawer to fit opening with 1/16″ clearance all around (use our dimensions as a guide). Glue false drawer front to front, overlapping evenly all around.

Stain all parts, following General Directions. Let dry and finish with polyurethane. Drill hole for and then screw on knob; attach hinges to back and edge of lid. Add wood plug after hanging.

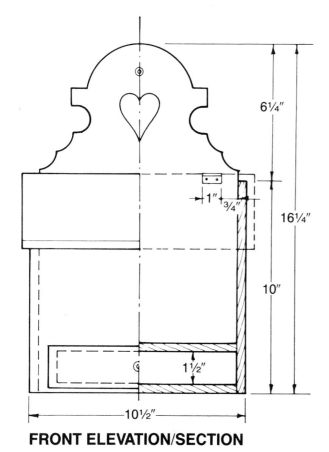

FRONT ELEVATION/SECTION

CROSS SECTION

75° angle

7¼″

drawer

5¾″

6¼″

6¼″

1″

¾″

16¼″

10″

1½″

10½″

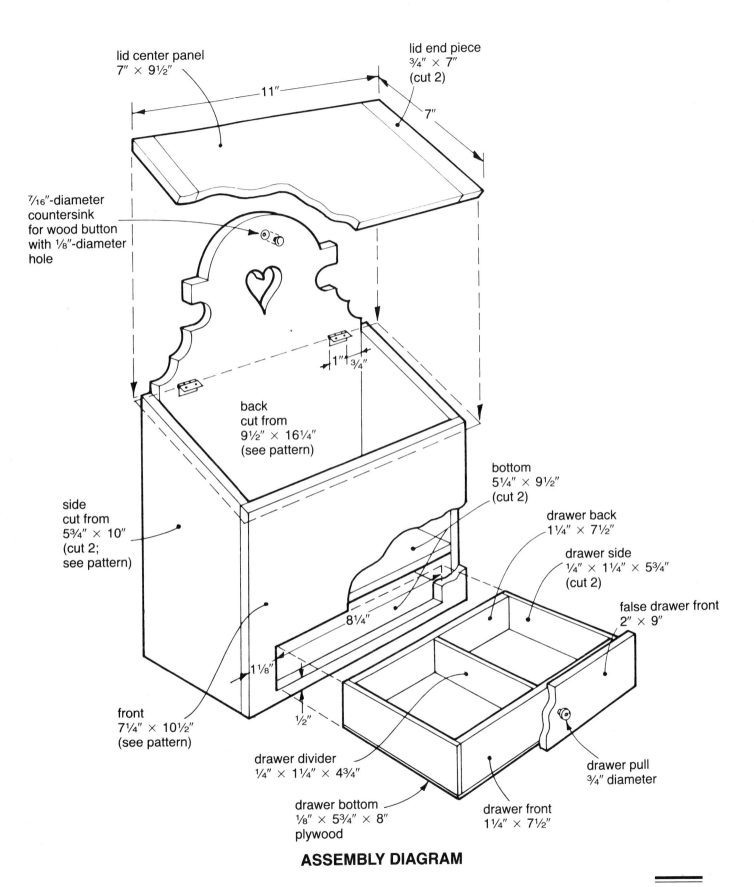

lid center panel
7″ × 9½″

lid end piece
¾″ × 7″
(cut 2)

11″

7″

⁷⁄₁₆″-diameter
countersink
for wood button
with ⅛″-diameter
hole

1″ ¾″

back
cut from
9½″ × 16¼″
(see pattern)

bottom
5¼″ × 9½″
(cut 2)

drawer back
1¼″ × 7½″

drawer side
¼″ × 1¼″ × 5¾″
(cut 2)

side
cut from
5¾″ × 10″
(cut 2;
see pattern)

false drawer front
2″ × 9″

8¼″

1⅛″

front
7¼″ × 10½″
(see pattern)

½″

drawer pull
¾″ diameter

drawer divider
¼″ × 1¼″ × 4¾″

drawer bottom
⅛″ × 5¾″ × 8″
plywood

drawer front
1¼″ × 7½″

ASSEMBLY DIAGRAM

COZY
BABY
CRADLE

*Here's a child's cradle so snug
and sweet it will rock your
baby to sleep as soon as he's
settled inside.*

SIZE:
Approximately 38″ long × 21″ high × 23″ wide

MATERIALS:
4′ × 6′ piece of ¾″ birch plywood
4′ of 2 × 6 clear pine for rockers
White glue
1½″ finishing nails
Six 2″ No. 10 flathead wood screws
Wood filler
Primer
Yellow nontoxic semigloss enamel
Purchased floral decals or packaged stencils

TOOLS:
Coping saw, drill, plane

Enlarge patterns for sides, head, foot, and rockers, following General Directions. Transfer patterns for sides, head, and foot pieces to ¾″ plywood; cut out.

To cut out hand grips on head and foot, drill one ¾″-diameter hole in each end of grips and cut out with coping saw. Following pattern for sides, bevel bottom edges of sides to 9° angle with plane. Fill and sand edges.

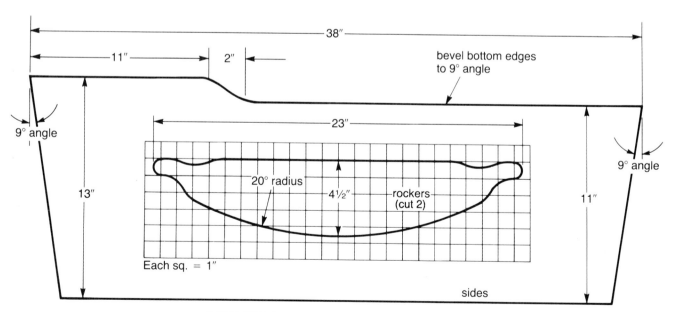

PATTERNS FOR ROCKERS AND SIDES

Glue and nail sides to head and foot as in assembly diagram. From remaining plywood, cut a floor piece to fit, beveling edges to match sides. Glue and nail floor in place.

Transfer pattern for rockers to 2 × 6 stock and cut out two rockers. To attach rockers, drill three holes across width of floor section 2½″ in from both ends and screw through floor.

Set and countersink all nail and screw heads; fill and sand smooth when dry. Apply two coats of primer, sanding lightly between coats; let dry. Apply two coats of enamel; let dry. Following manufacturer's directions, apply either stenciled motifs or decals to sides, head, and foot of cradle as in photograph.

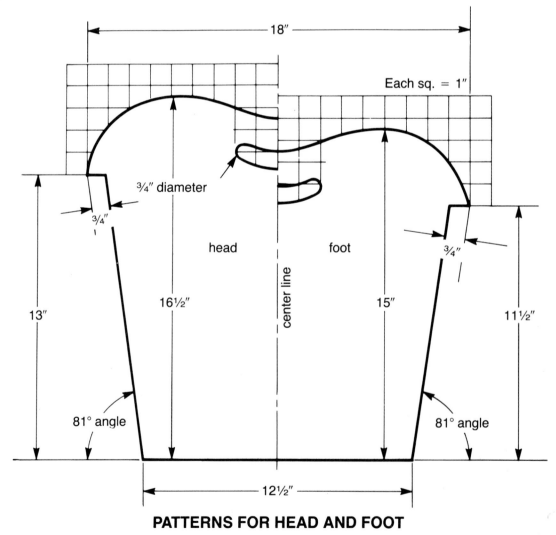

PATTERNS FOR HEAD AND FOOT

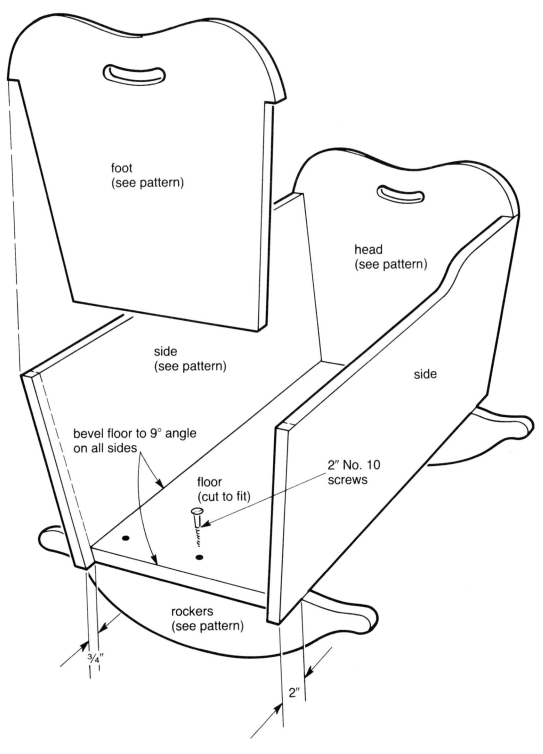

foot
(see pattern)

head
(see pattern)

side
(see pattern)

side

bevel floor to 9° angle
on all sides

2″ No. 10
screws

floor
(cut to fit)

rockers
(see pattern)

³/₄″

2″

ASSEMBLY DIAGRAM

FISHING-ROD RACK

Here's a special gift for the fisherman—or fisherwoman—in the family. It neatly holds an assortment of fishing rods and tackle in a handsome pine cabinet, forty-seven inches high. The fish decoration is cork—a reminder of all those others that didn't get away.

From 1 × 8 cut: two sides, 7″ × 47″; two drawer fronts and two backs, 4½″ × 11¼″; four drawer sides, 4½″ × 6″; three horizontal shelves, 6¼″ × 24½″; vertical divider, 4½″ × 6¼″.

Enlarge patterns, following General Directions; transfer to sides and shelf. Drill and saw out notches in shelf. For back, glue tongue-and-groove boards together as in diagram; follow pattern to cut curved top.

With rasp, round concave curved area of sides. Sand smooth.

Follow diagram for drawer section. Drill and countersink ends from the inside for No. 8 screws, and drill top for brass pulls. Nail top and bottom to vertical divider and ends. Screw drawer section between sides and attach recessed lattice strip. Glue and nail back into place. Glue and clamp notched shelf between sides and drill for dowels. Round dowel ends and glue into shelf so ends protrude slightly.

Each sq. = 1"

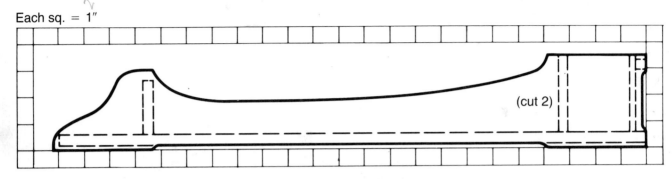

PATTERN FOR SIDES

(cut 2)

Each sq. = 1"

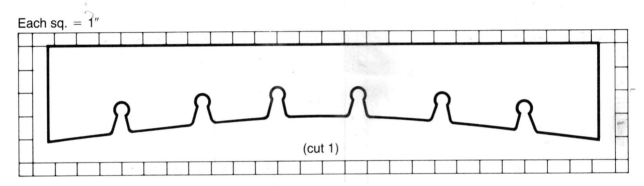

(cut 1)

PATTERN FOR NOTCHED SHELF

Each sq. = 1"

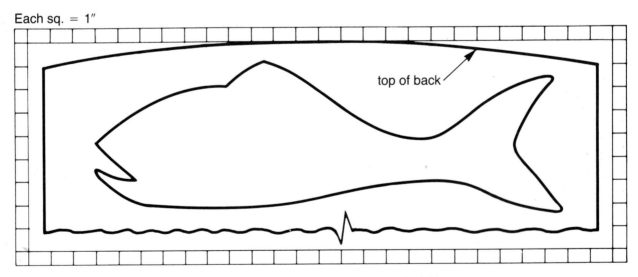

top of back

PATTERNS FOR BACK AND FISH

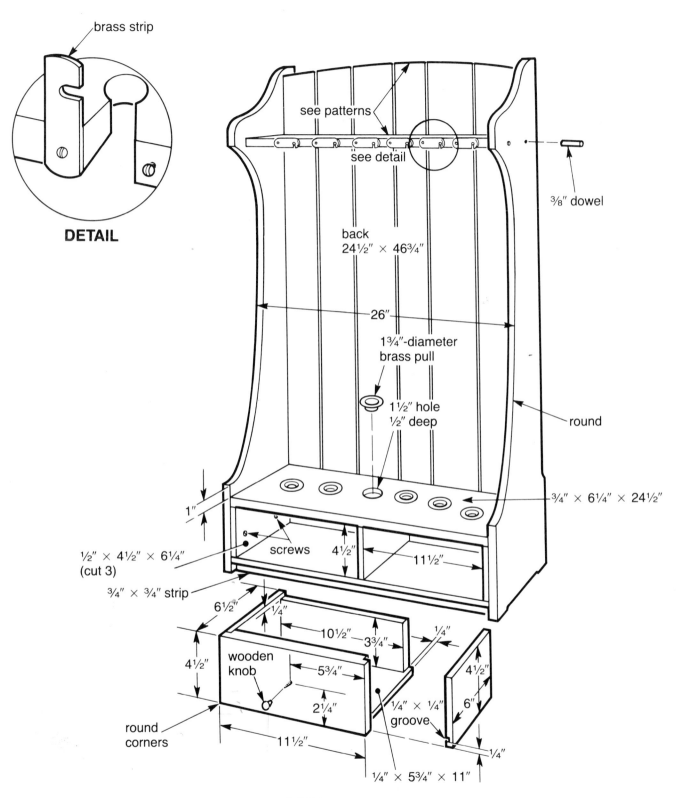

brass strip

DETAIL

see patterns

see detail

³⁄₈" dowel

back
24½" × 46¾"

26"

1¾"-diameter
brass pull

round

1½" hole
½" deep

1"

¾" × 6¼" × 24½"

½" × 4½" × 6¼"
(cut 3)

screws

4½"

11½"

¾" × ¾" strip

6½"

¼"

10½"   3¾"   ¼"

wooden
knob

5¾"

4½"

6"

¼"

2¼"

¼" × ¼"
groove

round
corners

11½"

¼" × 5¾" × 11"

ASSEMBLY DIAGRAM

To make drawers, cut pieces as in diagram, using hard-board for bottoms; rabbet fronts and sides and bottoms; groove sides. Assemble drawers with glue and brads. Drill for knobs.

Following detail, cut six brass strips for latches. Drill 5/32"-diameter holes in both ends of strips; saw out notch to go over screw at one end. Round strip ends with a file and apply clear lacquer. Drill shelf for 3/4" No. 6 roundhead brass screws. Sand all surfaces well and attach knobs. Apply antique pine finish, following General Directions. Let dry. Coat with polyurethane. Attach brass strips and glue brass pulls into shelf.

Follow pattern to cut fish from 1/4" bulletin-board cork. Stain fish with acrylic paint diluted with water and attach to back with white glue.

Note: The coping saw is used for cutting rounded notches. The saber saw is used for all other wood cuts. The hacksaw is used for cutting the brass strips.

FAMILY TREASURES

If you are the proud inheritor of some antiques your forebears collected or made, then you know what special dimensions such possessions add to a home.

If you would like to pass on a heritage of this sort to your own family, we offer three special pieces—not the easiest in the book, but not difficult, either, with our instructions.

CHILDREN'S TRESTLE TABLE AND CHAIRS

Here's a traditional Early American design that is not only timeless but sturdy enough to last for generations to come. The high-back chairs are practically tip-proof, and the child-resistant finish will protect the wood against years of rough-and-tumble play.

SIZES:

24″ wide × 14″ high × 16″ deep (table)

11¼″ wide × 22¼″ × 11″ deep (chair)

MATERIALS:

For trestle table:

   8′ of 1 × 10 No. 2 pine

   2″ No. 6 flathead wood screws

For chairs:

   13′ of 1 × 12 No. 2 pine

   1½″ finishing nails

For both:

   White glue

   Pine stain

   Polyurethane varnish

TOOLS:

Saber saw, drill with ¾″ spade bit, plane, clamp, sandpaper

For the table:

Following General Directions for joining boards for wider widths, cut two 8″ × 23″ pine pieces and join for table top. Trim both ends of joined boards to 22″.

Cut two 1″ × 16″ end pieces; glue and nail to ends of tabletop as in assembly diagram. Following diagram, mark and cut pieces for base from remaining pine.

Mark, predrill, and countersink all screw holes to assemble base and to attach tabletop. Assemble base with glue and screws, checking that base is square, then clamp until dry.

Sand base and tabletop smooth, rounding edges as in photograph. Attach base to top with screws as in diagram.

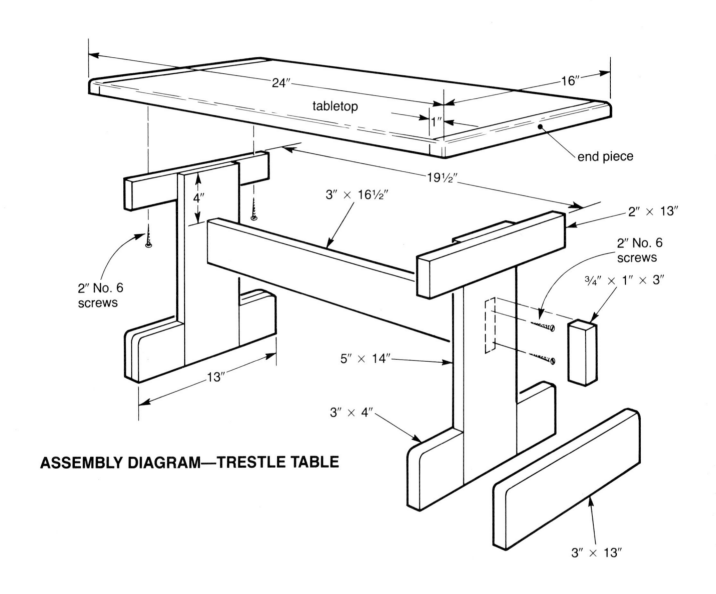

24"

16"

tabletop

1"

end piece

19½"

4"

3" × 16½"

2" × 13"

2" No. 6 screws

2" No. 6 screws

¾" × 1" × 3"

5" × 14"

13"

3" × 4"

3" × 13"

ASSEMBLY DIAGRAM—TRESTLE TABLE

For the chairs:

Enlarge pattern for chair sides, following General Directions. Transfer to wood. Cut sides with back edge beveled to 96° angle. (Plane beveled edge at a 6° angle.)

Following assembly diagram, mark and cut seat, back, and small triangular side pieces from remaining pine. For handhole in back piece, mark as indicated on diagram, then drill ends out with ¾″ spade bit; cut out wood between ends.

Sand chair pieces, rounding all edges that will not be joined. Assemble chairs as indicated with glue and nails. Apply stain to table and chairs, following General Directions. When dry, finish with two coats of polyurethane.

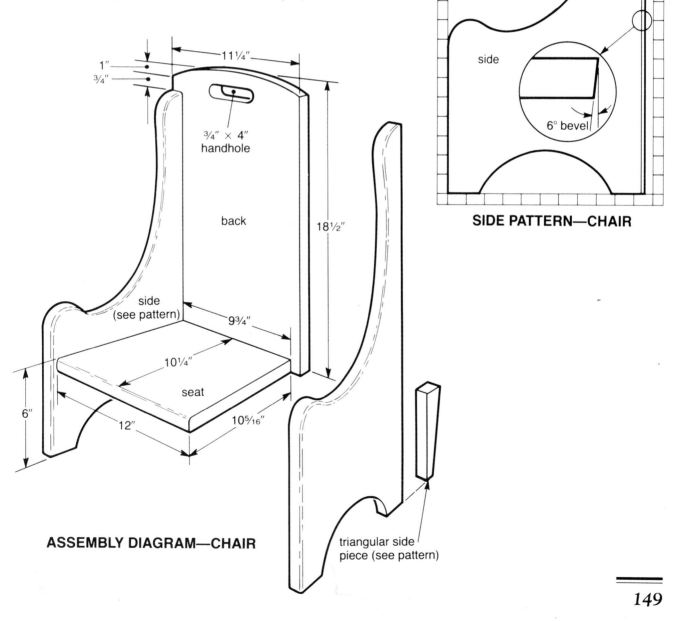

Each sq. = 1″

triangular side piece

side

6° bevel

SIDE PATTERN—CHAIR

11¼″

1″

¾″

¾″ × 4″ handhole

back

18½″

side (see pattern)

9¾″

10¼″

seat

6″

12″

10⁵⁄₁₆″

ASSEMBLY DIAGRAM—CHAIR

triangular side piece (see pattern)

A HANDSOME TWOSOME

These pieces are separate but work nicely as a pair. You might hang them both in the bathroom as a medicine cabinet and toothbrush shelf, or in a bedroom for all the little things that help a woman make herself beautiful. The cabinet has two shelves—enough to hide a multitude of secrets.

CABINET

Each sq. = ½″

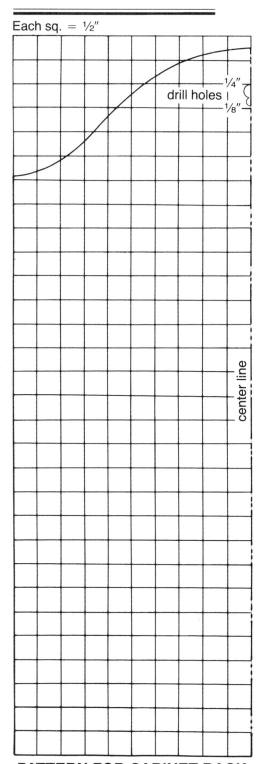

PATTERN FOR CABINET BACK

SIZE:
10¾″ wide × 14¾″ high × 5½″ deep

MATERIALS:
9′ of ½ × 6 clear pine
White glue
1″ brads
Two 1″ No. 4 roundhead wood screws
Two 1″ × 1″ brass-plated butt hinges with screws
Pine stain
½″-diameter wooden knob
Polyurethane varnish
Paste wax

TOOLS:
Drill, saber saw, clamp, chisel, sandpaper, steel wool

Following General Directions, join board widths for back and door pieces. Enlarge pattern for back, transfer shape to pine, and cut out. Mark and drill double hole to hang cabinet as indicated.

From remaining pine, cut bottom, top, sides, jambs, and shelf pieces as indicated in the assembly diagram. Be certain to cut sides and jambs to length at the same time.

Begin assembling cabinet as in diagram. Glue and nail jambs to sides; add bottom, then insert shelf between sides. Glue and nail back in place with bottom flush at back edge and extending ⅜″ at sides, then attach top flush against back edge and extending ⅜″ at sides.

Cut two ⅜″ × ½″ × ½″ filler blocks. Glue in place at top and bottom back edges as indicated.

From pieced pine, cut door, allowing enough clearance for it to swing freely. Cut shaped latch as indicated and predrill screw hole for latch on jamb. Mortise door and cabinet for hinges and attach. Drill door for wooden knob.

Sand cabinet smooth, rounding edges (do not fill). Apply stain, following General Directions. When dry, finish with polyurethane and paste wax.

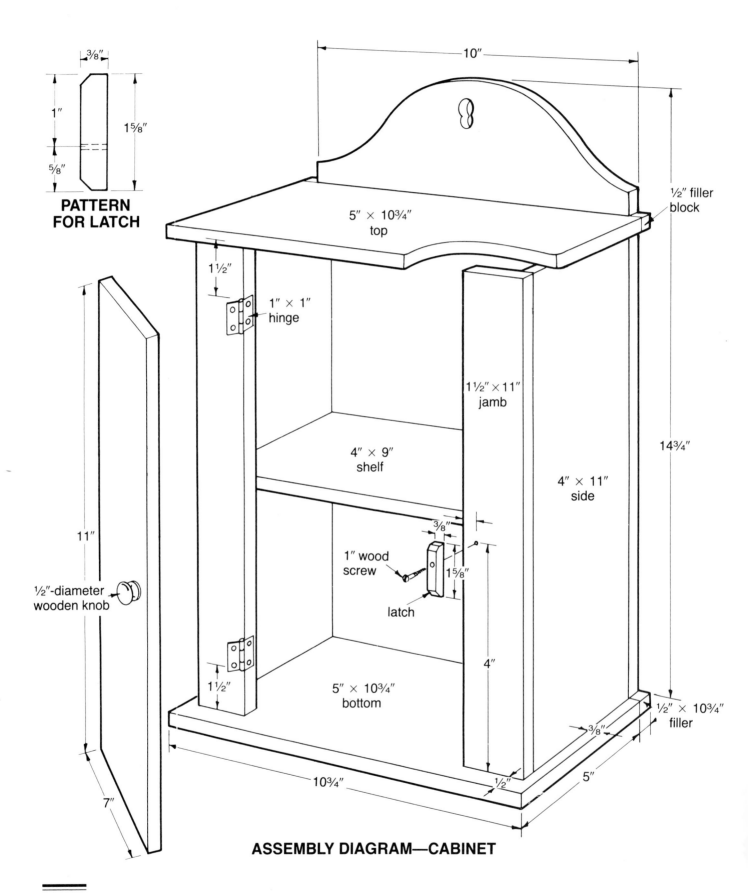

**PATTERN
FOR LATCH**

3/8″

1″

1 5/8″

5/8″

10″

1/2″ filler
block

5″ × 10 3/4″
top

1 1/2″

1″ × 1″
hinge

1 1/2″ × 11″
jamb

14 3/4″

4″ × 9″
shelf

4″ × 11″
side

11″

3/8″

1″ wood
screw

1 5/8″

latch

1/2″-diameter
wooden knob

4″

1 1/2″

5″ × 10 3/4″
bottom

1/2″ × 10 3/4″
filler

3/8″

7″

10 3/4″

1/2″

5″

ASSEMBLY DIAGRAM—CABINET

RACK

SIZE:
14" wide × 4" high × 3" deep

MATERIALS:
3' of ½ × 6 clear pine
White glue
Pine stain
1" brads
Polyurethane varnish
Paste wax

TOOLS:
Drill, saw, sandpaper, rasp, steel wool

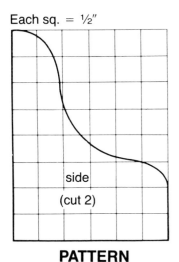

Each sq. = ½"

side

(cut 2)

**PATTERN
FOR RACK SIDE**

Enlarge pattern for sides, following General Directions. Mark and cut two shaped sides at one time. Cut back, bottom, and front pieces as indicated on the assembly diagram. Mark and drill two ¼"-diameter holes in back for hanging rack.

Assemble rack with glue and nails; add sides to front and back, then insert bottom. Round top front edge with rasp to match curve of sides; sand rack smooth. Apply stain. When dry, finish with polyurethane and paste wax, following General Directions.

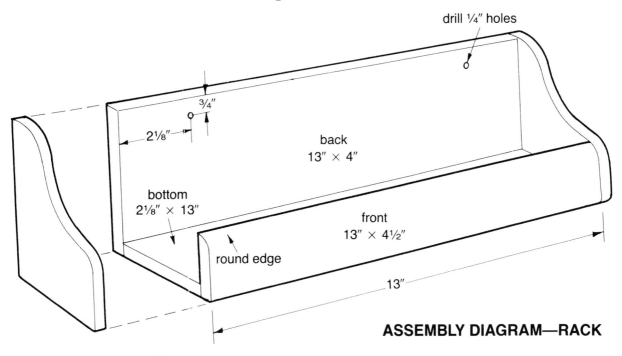

drill ¼" holes

¾"

2⅛"

back
13" × 4"

bottom
2⅛" × 13"

round edge

front
13" × 4½"

13"

ASSEMBLY DIAGRAM—RACK

DRESSING
TABLE
CADDY

Most everyone can use another mirror in the house, especially if it comes along with a small drawer to store all those what-nots you never know where to hide. The mirror, held by dowels, lifts out so you can use it anywhere you like, and the drawer can easily be partitioned to the size of the items you need to store.

SIZE:
Mirror and Stand: 11¼″ wide × 13½″ high × 2¾″ deep
Caddy: 12¾″ wide × 3¾″ high × 8¾″ deep

MATERIALS:
5′ of ½ × 10 clear pine
2′ of 1 × 1 clear pine
3′ of ¼″ × ½″ lattice
1′ of ¼″ × 1⅜″ lattice
3′ of ½″ × ¾″ lattice
1′ of ½″ × 1⅝″ lattice
White glue
1″ brads
⅛″ and ½″ dowels
2′ × 2′ piece of ⅛″ hardboard
¼″ mirror to fit
Pine stain
Polyurethane varnish
Paste wax

TOOLS:
Saber saw, drill, sandpaper, plane

From ½ × 10 pine, cut for the caddy: two sides, 2¾″ × 8″; bottom, 8¾″ × 12¾″; top, 8½″ × 12″; back, 2¾″ × 11″.

Referring to the assembly diagram, glue and nail sides to back. Keeping top and bottom flush to back, glue and nail. Bottom will extend ⅜″ at sides and ¾″ at front.

From 1 × 1 pine, cut two 10″ mirror posts. Drill ⅛″-diameter holes in posts for dowel pivots, as indicated. Use a plane to taper posts.

From ½ × 10 pine, cut for mirror stand: base, 2¾″ × 11¼″; stretcher, 1″ × 7½″ (taper ends to fit posts).

Glue and nail posts to stretcher as shown; next, centering mirror stand on base piece, glue then nail in place from underneath. Glue base piece with stand in place on top of caddy ⅜″ in from back and side edges.

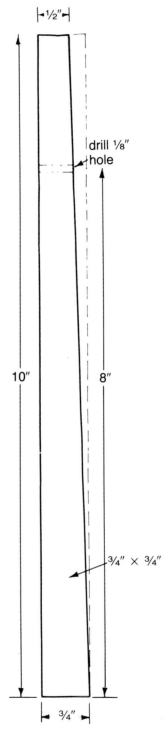

PATTERN FOR MIRROR POSTS

The mirror is made from three layers. The outer layer, which forms the frame, is made from ½″ lattice; the middle layer, which forms the rabbet, is made from ¼″ lattice; and the back is made from ⅛″ hardboard.

Following construction detail, cut lattice for mirror frame. Shape top pieces of frame following pattern. Assemble mirror frame with glue; when dry, trim and sand all edges flush, slightly rounding them. Drill holes in frame sides lined up with ⅛″ holes drilled in posts for pivot.

From remaining ½ × 10 pine and ⅛″ hardboard, cut drawer pieces. Rabbet drawer sides for hardboard bottom. Test-assemble drawer and check that there is enough clearance so that drawer slides into caddy easily. Assemble drawer with glue and nails. Cut ½″ dowel for drawer pulls, shaped as indicated. Also cut ⅛″ dowel for mirror pivots.

Sand dressing caddy and mirror frame smooth. Following General Directions, distress caddy if desired, then apply stain. Let dry. Finish with coat of polyurethane.

Cut hardboard back ⅛″ smaller all around than frame. Insert mirror and nail or screw hardboard to back. Hang mirror in stand with dowel pivots as shown.

Each sq. = ½″

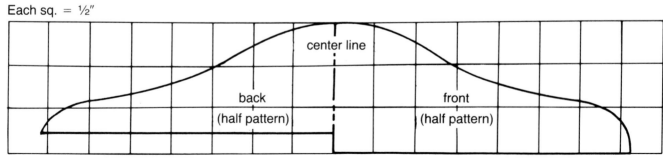

center line

back
(half pattern)

front
(half pattern)

PATTERNS FOR TOP OF MIRROR FRAME

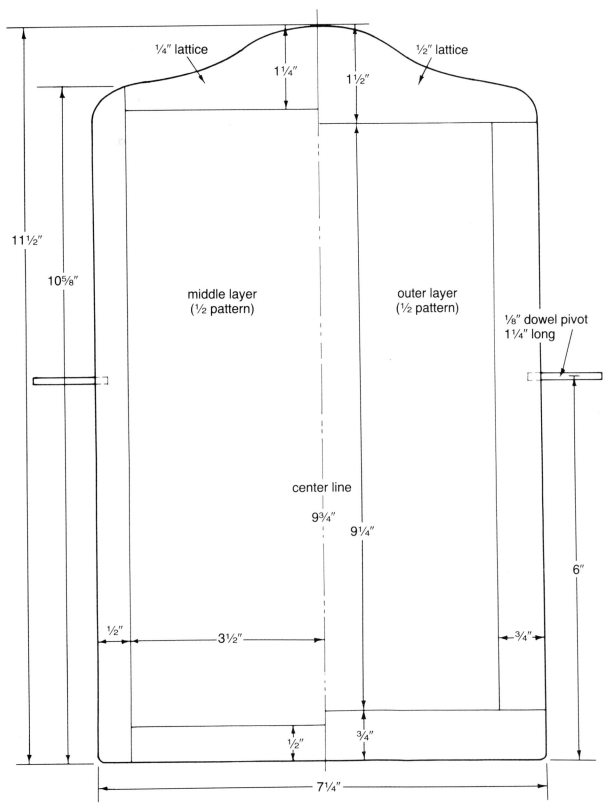

CONSTRUCTION DETAIL OF MIRROR FRAME

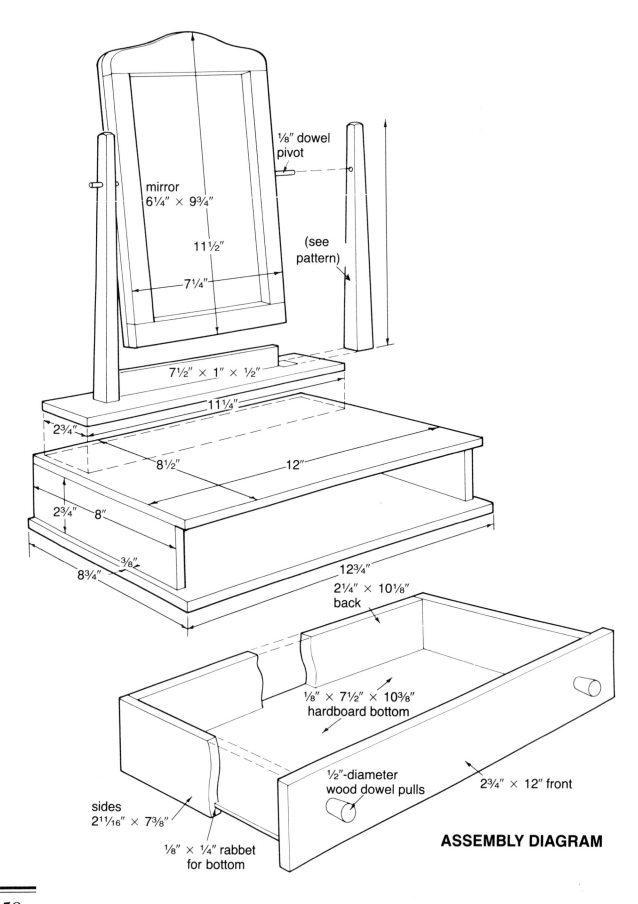

1/8" dowel
pivot

mirror
6 1/4" × 9 3/4"

11 1/2"

7 1/4"

(see
pattern)

7 1/2" × 1" × 1/2"

11 1/4"

2 3/4"

8 1/2"

12"

2 3/4"   8"

3/8"

8 3/4"

12 3/4"

2 1/4" × 10 1/8"
back

1/8" × 7 1/2" × 10 3/8"
hardboard bottom

1/2"-diameter
wood dowel pulls

2 3/4" × 12" front

sides
2 11/16" × 7 3/8"

1/8" × 1/4" rabbet
for bottom

ASSEMBLY DIAGRAM

GENERAL
DIRECTIONS

To Enlarge Patterns to Full Size: You will need brown wrapping paper (pieced if necessary, to make a large enough sheet for a pattern), a felt-tipped marker, pencil, and ruler. (*Note:* If pattern you are enlarging has grid line around it, first connect lines across pattern with a colored pencil to form a grid over the picture. At the proper enlargement, each square will equal the measure indicated on the pattern.) Mark paper with grid as follows:

First cut your paper into a true square or rectangle. Then mark dots 1″ or 2″ apart, or whatever is indicated on pattern, around edges, making same number of spaces as there are squares around the edges of the pattern diagram. Form a grid by joining the dots across opposite sides of the paper. Check to make sure you have the same number of squares as shown in the diagram. With a marker, draw in each square the same pattern lines you see in the corresponding square on the diagram.

Transferring and Shaping Patterns: Enlarge patterns on brown paper, then transfer to material with carbon paper. When a half pattern is given, draw a center line on the wood, using a square. Flop pattern to transfer other side of design. (To do this, you may want to trace the half pattern onto tracing paper large enough to cover design.)

Cutting Tools—Saws: Many of the projects in this book are cut with either a saber or coping saw. The saber saw, a small power tool, can be used throughout for all straight cuts, as can a handsaw. The saber saw will also cut curves and interior shapes. The coping saw is almost always used for the more decorative work (such as the Marmalade Cat Mug Holder) and also for interior cuts. It is hardly, if ever, used for straight cutting. A hacksaw is used for cutting metals such as the brass strips for the Fishing-Rod Rack. Other handsaws such as a bucksaw can be used for mitering moldings and frames. A circular saw, which is a power tool, can be used for straight cuts, mitering, and angling, but be sure that the work to be cut is supported so that it will not shift during the cut.

Preparing and Cutting Materials: To assure accuracy and avoid errors, do not cut all parts at one time, but follow the sequence described in the instructions and diagrams. When cutting, be sure to leave enough material to plane the saw cuts. Pieces that are identical should be cut at one time. To do this, temporarily nail pieces together outside cutting lines. *To cut openings* (such as the heart in the oak rocker or oval in the step stool), mark outline on wood, then drill one or two holes inside the line and saw with a coping or saber saw; file and sand to shape.

Dowels: Test-fit dowels in holes drilled in scrap wood first to ensure an accurate fit. Clamp and drill matching pieces at one time. To provide a starter hole for bit, use a center punch or awl. Clamp a scrap of wood to the back of pieces being drilled to prevent splintering. Mark center of dowel hole on wood. Use an adjustable bit gauge where specified to mark for depth, and use a doweling jig (if you have one) to drill on center. Cut lengthwise groove in dowel and glue into hole. Wipe off excess glue and sand end flush.

Wood Measures: All of the pine projects in this book are made from clear pine unless otherwise stated. When purchasing stock, remember that the actual dimensions of the wood will be less than the standard stated size (e.g., 1 × 8 will measure ¾″ × 7⅝″, and so on).

Joining Boards for Width: When a part is wider than the width of boards available, two or more pieces should be edge-glued together. Use white glue—waterproof, if you are working on an outdoor piece. This technique also prevents most warping, which occurs in very wide boards. To edge-glue, plane edges so they fit very tightly against each other, particularly at the ends of the boards, which tend to shrink more than the centers. Always test-fit before gluing. Apply glue to edges and place pipe clamps across top and bottom of boards. Remove squeezed-out glue with damp cloth. Let dry. Mark with a square and cut to exact size. If exposed surface is uneven, plane where joined.

To Notch or Mortise: Mark wood. Use a saw to cut across the grain, then gradually remove waste wood with a chisel. For hinges, mark size and chisel out recess deep enough to accommodate thickness of metal.

To Rabbet: Mark each edge to be cut. Saw each side to required depth and chisel out excess wood.

To Bevel and Round: To bevel, plane edge to required angle. Round edges with a rasp and sandpaper. Do this before assembling wherever possible.

Nailing and Screwing: Use finishing nails for thick wood, brads for thin. When attaching layers of wood, be sure nails or brads are at least ⅛″ shorter than the combined thicknesses of wood. After nailing, set the nail head slightly. When using a screw, countersink it by first drilling the hole ⅛″ deeper than the length of the screw itself.

Preparation for Finishing: Use spackling compound to fill defects and nail and screw holes on surfaces to be painted. Fill holes on surfaces to be stained with matching wood filler. To obtain a good finish, surfaces must be sanded as smooth as possible. This is particularly important when a piece is to be stained. Always sand *with* the grain. In general, use progressively finer grits of sandpaper, beginning with medium, then fine, and finishing with very fine. For best results, use a sanding block. Your paper will frequently gum up with resin when sanding pine, so replace the paper when this happens. Slapping dust out of your sandpaper will make it last longer. Always dust thoroughly before staining or priming, using a vacuum and a tack cloth.

To Stain: Stains must be stirred before using and during application to distribute the color ingredients evenly. They are generally applied with a rag or brush, and then wiped with a cloth to remove excess and provide a uniform color. This may vary slightly with different products, so read and follow the manufacturer's directions.

Apply stain thinly and evenly, following the grain. Do not slap it on haphazardly; avoid drip streaks. Work on one surface at a time, choosing less conspicuous areas to do first and leaving tops and fronts for last. If you want a lighter shade, you must be ready to wipe quickly, always working with the grain. The longer you let a stain remain on the surface before wiping, the deeper it will soak in and the darker your finish will be. *Tip:* Use steel wool instead of sandpaper to smooth the surface, and apply a second coat of stain for a highly professional finish.

If the wood is fairly uniform in color but the stain does not penetrate evenly, allow the stain to remain longer on the less absorbent areas, and wipe quickly where it sinks in more rapidly.

Most stained surfaces dry to a dull, lifeless finish that requires the protection of varnish. Most of the pieces in this book are finished with two coats of satin-finish polyurethane varnish, sanded in between coats with superfine sandpaper. Some pieces are then coated with paste wax and buffed with a soft cloth when dry.

Note: Artist's acrylic, when diluted with water, works as a stain. It is necessary to sand between each application.

Antique Pine Finish: Apply stain as above. When dry, thin burnt umber paint with stain and apply to corners and edges of piece. Let stand for five minutes and rub to blend into stain. Follow with a coat of satin-finish polyurethane varnish; let dry thoroughly for at least eight hours. Sand lightly and apply a second coat. Apply paste wax with fine-grade steel wool. Buff with a soft dry cloth.

Distressing: To achieve a further antiqued look, beat the wood with a heavy chain or heat the point of a finishing nail over a flame and tap the nail partially into the wood surface. Remove by rotating the nail in the wood rather than by pulling up, to avoid wood whiskers. Create an irregular grouping of holes and dents for a more authentic look. You can also hammer dents. Stain and finish.

Paint Finish: Fill and sand wood thoroughly, following instructions on Preparation for Finishing (see page 163). Apply two coats white shellac primer thinned with 50-50 denatured alcohol. (This type of primer is used on every project requiring primer.) Sand with fine sandpaper in between coats. The surface is now ready to be painted a solid color or stenciled. Enamel or acrylic paint can be used. One can also finish a piece by simply priming it this way. A final coat of polyurethane protects it. Satin-finish polyurethane is used on every project, painted or stained, requiring a final finish.

Antiquing: One can also antique a primed or painted surface with thinned-out burnt umber or burnt sienna paint (thinned out with 2 ounces of water to ½ teaspoon of paint). Stroke on painted surface, then wipe off excess with paper towel. Distressing the piece for a further antiqued look can also be done before or after painting. Finish with two coats satin polyurethane and paste wax if desired.

Outdoor Projects: Use waterproof glue, plastic wood filler, and exterior primer before painting, and at least two coats of polyurethane varnish for protection.

Stenciling: Place clear-seal adhesive vinyl or plastic (such as Contact®), including backing, faceup over enlarged pattern (hold against window or light box if lines do not show through), and draw design on front of stencil with marker. Cut out with a craft knife. Remove backing and press stencil to wood. For most pieces the negative image is used and you paint through the opening. For others, the positive image is used to block out the shape while you paint the background. Dab acrylic paint through the stencil with a sponge or a stencil brush held perpendicular to the surface. Referring to the color photographs, paint areas either solid or shaded, depending on the finish required. Remove stencil when paint is completely dry. If design includes more than one color, repeat as required with each stencil. Finish pieces according to individual instructions.

Hanging: Many projects require a sawtooth hanger tacked to the back; others have a small hole drilled in one or two spots or can be nailed or screwed directly to the wall.

Index